Fit
MAMA

This book is dedicated to all the women who are living the 'mum life' and trying to be true to themselves; to those who are doing their best, even when they feel like they are failing; to the women who cry; to the women who try; to the women who refuse to apologise for who they are and who they're striving to be; to the women who are strong, and to those who are just discovering their strength; to the real women who make mistakes; to those who, no matter what, will not give up; to all the women who are scared; and to those trying to figure out how to do it right.

Love yourself. Trust your instincts. You are enough. You really are beautiful in every single way.

Health and happiness, always.

b.x

Fit MAMA

GET THE BEST BODY YOU'VE EVER HAD ... AFTER KIDS

Belinda Norton

MURDOCH BOOKS

SYDNEY · LONDON

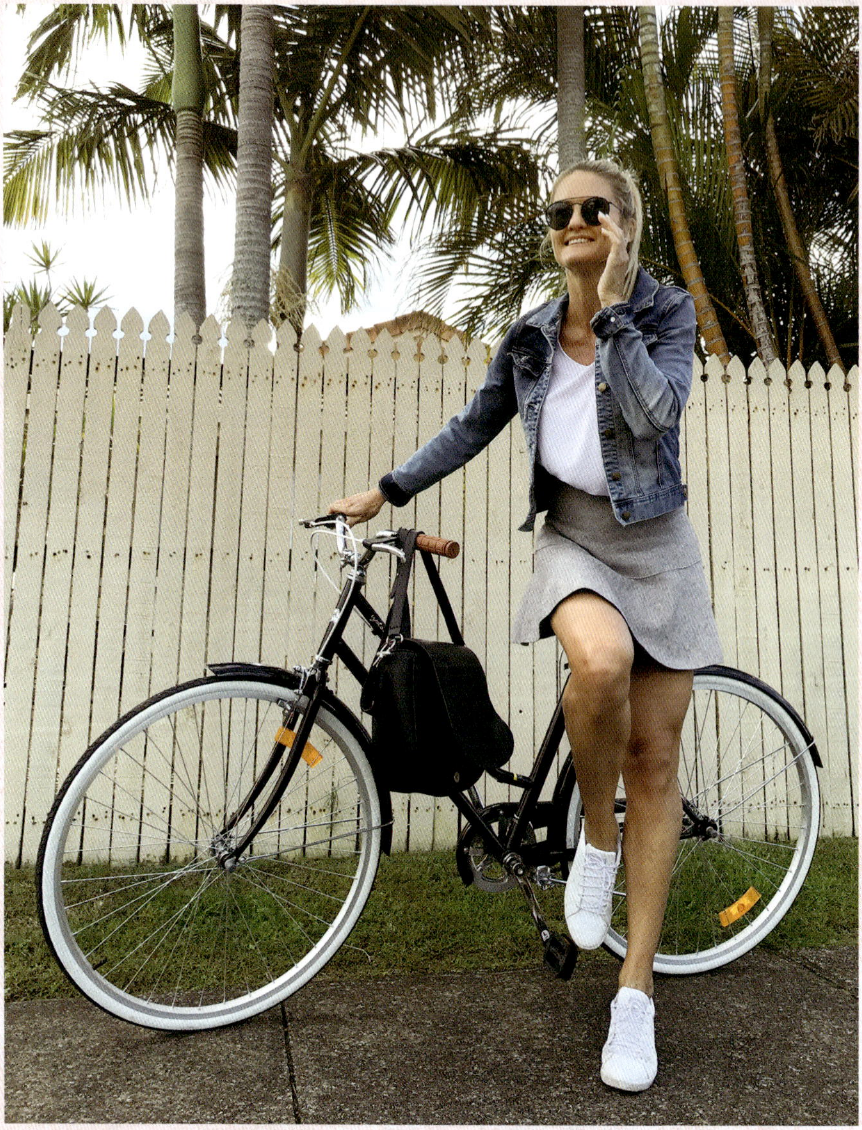

Contents

INTRODUCTION 6

1
Becoming a mum
WHAT HAPPENED TO MY BODY? 8

2
Plan your new life
PRACTICAL TIPS TO MAKE IT WORK 30

3
Find your strength
THE ABC OF GETTING FIT 44

4
Find your confidence
CHANGE YOUR RELATIONSHIP WITH FOOD AND YOUR BODY 68

5
Find your balance
MIND OVER MATTER 96

6
Fit Mama fitness
TIME TO STEP UP 114

7
Fit Mama fuel
HEALTHY RECIPES FOR BUSY FAMILIES 144

THANKS 204

INDEX 205

We are all doing our best. Some of us are mums who hardly have time to get dressed and barely get any sleep. Some of us are caring for ageing parents or a houseful of pets while also juggling a career. There are only 24 hours in a day: who has time for exercise?

The fact is, we all do. And it's not just about trimming down or toning up, it's about taking care of ourselves mentally and physically so we can function at our best.

Being a single working mum of two growing children, I know how important it is to get things done quickly and well. I also know how defeating it can feel to dislike your post-child body, to feel out of shape and overtired, to no longer feel comfortable in your own skin.

My personal transformation from frumpy to fit after having children involved not only a physical transformation, but a mental and emotional one, too. People say that getting fit will not make you happy, but I totally disagree. I was happy before, but getting fit allowed me to discover a whole new level of happiness and a sense of wellbeing. I never have to bargain with myself to exercise, and I never have that 'oh, I wish I hadn't …' feeling. As I wrote this book, my goal was to offer a path that felt possible, inspiring and motivating for anyone who wants to turn back the clock and feel fit and gorgeous again after having children.

The Fit Mama program is designed to be achievable within a busy and demanding lifestyle. There are bodyweight exercises that can be completed on the go; simple food advice, recipes and menus; tips for organising your time; and easy-to-follow workout plans. It is an inspirational, body-positive and practical training and eating plan to get you moving and feeling great.

I have always been involved in fitness one way or another. From my days as a triathlon competitor to teaching children PE, becoming a fitness expert has helped me overcome most of the difficulties in my life, from the trauma of birth to hormonal imbalances and postnatal depression — and I wanted to share this insight with others. In particular, I wanted to remove the guesswork for mothers, sharing simple food; easy, accessible workouts and good nutritional information. This is my way of helping women make good, sustainable lifestyle choices to improve mobility, confidence and energy. It's about encouraging you to discover the best version of yourself, both for yourself and your family.

I am grateful for the life I lead, for the steps I have taken to be where I am now and for the opportunity to help others.

The best way to describe my life now is 'complete'. I feel happy with my body and have devised a way to keep my fitness on track. I don't fear food, or my choices around food, because I have found a way of eating that works for me. I hardly ever get sick and I barely use any medications, which means I'm able to spend this money on other things, such as great produce and interesting new ingredients that excite my family.

Family life is easier now, too. We all know exactly what we are eating, so there is no guesswork. I set up weekly menus on a two-week rotation and add new recipes every six months. This might sound boring, but it makes life so much easier and, when we are in the mood for something new, we go out to a restaurant or I find new recipes to try out.

Countless people transform their bodies, but the ones who do it successfully focus on health, energy and longevity. They find ways to train and ways to eat that suit their lives, and they stick to them. Simply focusing on nourishing the body and eating wholefoods that feel good becomes addictive in its own way. The better we nourish ourselves and our families, the better we function, giving us the confidence to overcome life's challenges and feel happy and energised while doing it.

Once you are armed with the information you need to train and eat like a Fit Mama, you'll have the tools to go forwards and achieve the kind of body you have always dreamed of. This life is for living, and living well. And now is the time to put your fears, distractions and excuses aside and commit to working towards a happier and healthier future. It won't always be easy, but it is definitely worth it and, before long, you will be enjoying your new-found energy, vibrancy and a healthier outlook on life. I promise, you won't look back.

I want you to achieve your most enviable body transformation. Are you with me?

Belinda

1

Becoming a mum

WHAT HAPPENED TO MY BODY?

I, too, have been where you are right now: stuck in a post-baby body rut that is hanging around a little longer than you expected.

I was happy, but tired. I was self-conscious, but still tried to make others around me laugh. I worked as hard as I could, providing for my two children, tending to household chores and working full-time. I was the same person that I am today, but I often felt dreadfully upset with myself for the poor choices I made and the excuses I gave. Do you know anyone like that?

Even when we know things have changed, we often hide from our own truth. I know I did. When my thighs rubbed together and chafed, I bought longer denim shorts to cover them. When my tummy sagged over the top of my jeans, I pulled them up higher to hide it. I even changed my hair colour in the hope of concealing my disappointment with my body, going from short, cropped blonde hair to red hair and then brown with blonde tips—even a bob cut with bangs (a bad idea, considering my face shape).

I was moody and lethargic, and it began to affect my family life until, one day, I decided I'd had enough.

The story goes like this: I was sitting on the floor in front of my now-ex-husband, and I showed him a photo of a girl on social media. She was fit, lean and had phenomenal posture. She looked strong, but feminine. I said, 'Oh, I wish I could look like that.'

'You could train day and night and you would never look like that,' he scoffed. That was the sentence that lit a fire in my belly.

Doubters have always spurred me on. My own brothers used to use this tactic to provoke me to fight with them. I was born and bred in the bayside suburbs of Brisbane and always had a wholesome coastal lifestyle in my sights. As a young girl, I developed a strong work ethic: a virtue I cultivated as an adult, especially in my fitness training. Over the years, however—particularly after having

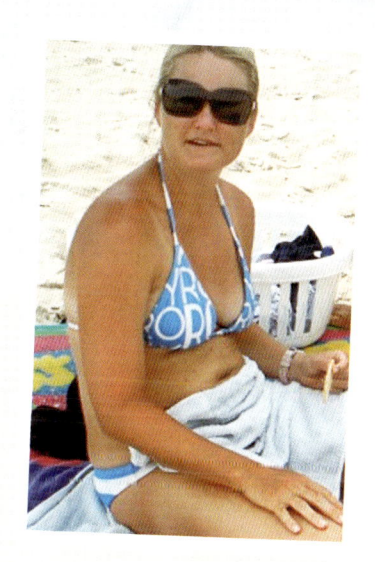

My post-baby bod

children—I began to lose my drive and desire to succeed. I tried to maintain my old fitness regime, but it was no longer working. I overdid the cardio, causing my metabolism to become sluggish. Soon, I succumbed to reaching for fast food and sugary snacks. I ate the kids' leftovers. I told myself that, despite these mistakes, I was 'pretty good most of the time'.

Do you say that to yourself? 'I'm pretty good most of the time.' Do you go over what you ate in your head, counting up that tiny high-sugar cake, the leftover biscuits, the few sips of Coke and that handful of hot chips, thinking, 'I ran a slow 12 kilometres this morning, but at least I did it'? Yeah, me too. I said those things to myself and to others, but it was not until I stopped the 'little bits' and the 'pretty good' eating and focused on training that my health and overall mobility improved.

No one could do this for me, only me. Only I could change my habits and, from now on, I was going to be consistent with my food choices and fitness routines. I'd get real information and follow it exactly. I'd literally had a gutful of my gut and thighs.

THE STEPS I FOLLOWED WERE PRETTY STRAIGHTFORWARD:

STEP 1: Set a food regime.
STEP 2: Correct my fitness.
STEP 3: Be consistent and goal-focused.
STEP 4: Include personal rewards (such as a facial or a massage, *not* chocolate).

Being truthful with yourself is difficult. It's easy to make excuses and then repeat them to others in the hope that they will agree. But what really matters is how you feel, not what they think. How does your body function? Are you mobile and maintaining energy? Are you often sick? Are you moody, or do you have a positive outlook on life? Recognising your body's signals—and alarm bells—is the first step towards reclaiming it, and I will show you how to do it using the Fit Mama program.

Becoming a mum 11

Where it all began

To understand how I changed my mindset and body, you need to know how it all started. I have two brothers who are both intellectually gifted and have impressive athletic abilities. They taught me the meaning of strength and how to take it to the next level. I didn't fall into an athletic lifestyle by chance; I was forced to embrace it growing up. I would ride my bike to school, even in the driving rain, wearing my long, bottle-green skirt and blouse, and balancing a heavy schoolbag on the bag rack. I would race my brothers to and from school every single day. My older brother always won, but my younger brother and I never stopped trying. (I think this is where my competitiveness comes from.) I look back fondly on those days, as they were just about the simple joy of moving our bodies and having fun. Exercise was enjoyable and effortless. After having children, I lost the joy I had felt playing sport and came to see it only as a chore. I went off track.

Looking back, the sport that brought me the greatest enjoyment and personal success was the triathlon. In my school years, I was a member of many different sports teams, but it was the triathlon that fulfilled my love of endurance training and immersed me in my favourite disciplines: swimming, cycling and running.

This sport became more than just a hobby. I began doing local races in Brisbane and the Gold Coast, then started competing in racing events around Australia. I particularly enjoyed the longer races, such as the Half Ironman. (Sprinting wasn't really my thing; I just didn't have the speed.) The demands of my training became evident to my lecturers and tutors, and they suggested that I apply for support so I could continue training and studying at Griffith University, especially as I had just graduated to Ironman triathlons. I was granted a sport scholarship to complete my Health and Physical Education degree. Now I could concentrate on making one of my many dreams come true: being a professional triathlete.

Swimming as a child ignited my passion for sport

My triathlon days

After moving to the Gold Coast, I was keen to continue my training, and what better way to do that than with a group? I have such fond, fun memories of the triathlon squad from the few years that I trained with them. It is also where I met my best friend, Emma Snowsill-Frodeno. I loved watching her go on to hit the world stage and compete at the highest level. I yearned for this, too, but while I had great self-discipline when it came to training, I was never the best racer.

The greatest takeaways from my years of triathlons were the friendships and the vast amount of knowledge that I absorbed from my many coaches, medical experts and mentors. I loved to learn about the scientific details of our bodies, and our coaches often trained with us, discussing functional body tips and the importance of maintaining optimum fitness. These athletes, coaches and experts shared so much valuable information with us, and I want to share it with you in this book.

These experts—who include sports scientists, conditioning coaches, physiotherapists, alignment specialists and nutritionists, many of whom have achieved great success in the world of sport—shaped me, not only as a triathlete, but as a person, too. I was truly blessed to spend time with them on a daily basis, and I am still mentored by many of them today.

Becoming a mum

Training and pregnancy

Working full-time teaching physical education to children, running personal training sessions and years of competing in triathlons left my body in disarray. The intense training required for triathlons and the resulting injuries meant that my body was always out of balance. I was mentally exhausted and had not had a period in years. In an effort to correct this imbalance and improve my fertility, I decided to cut back on my training, focusing on shorter, local races instead of triathlons. My periods eventually returned, but they were very irregular. After consulting with a naturopath, I tried cutting out dairy and altering my food intake. It took two years of trying before I actually fell pregnant.

Pregnancy was not my finest moment. I laugh now, but at the time it wasn't funny at all. I was teaching at a school on the northern end of the Gold Coast, and every single day I vomited on waking, after showering and on my way to work. The only things that seemed to stay down were toasted ham and cheese sandwiches and chocolate milk. I have not touched either since.

My son decided to come two weeks before his due date and goodness, I was not ready. In my training I thrived on challenges and had made pain my friend, so surely this wouldn't be any different? How wrong I was. I can't really remember anything but white lights. Many women tell of their vision of white lights while giving birth: I believe they are meeting their ultimate pain threshold. I have seen these white lights a few times, not just in childbirth but also while racing. It's as if hitting a new level of pain causes the brain to switch off—everything goes foggy and white.

Two years later, the birth of my daughter was also tough. Labour started right on schedule, but she was in no rush to come out. I was in so much pain that I pushed my fists tightly into my eye sockets, giving myself two black eyes. I had gone into both births thinking I'd be all right, that I was fit and strong and that it would be a breeze. As it turned out, my daughter's birth was even harder than my son's—something I wouldn't have believed possible.

In the birthing suite with my second child

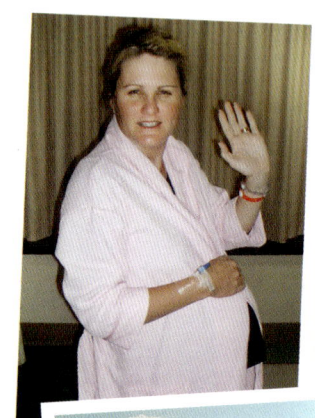

Afterwards, the struggles of motherhood were draining. I felt overwhelmed and out of control. I was always tired and worried about nourishing my children properly. The physical demands of breastfeeding and the roller-coaster ride of hormones made it even harder but, slowly, I settled into some kind of a groove, balancing working life with motherhood.

After a couple of weeks, it was time to get moving again and restart some training. In hindsight, I returned to exercise much too soon. I was in a rush to get my pre-baby body back and went straight into running. Of course, my delicate pelvis was still healing, and I soon noticed that I wasn't making the gains I had expected. I sought advice from various health professionals and educated myself. Exercise alone was not enough; I had to cleanse my body from the inside out. I slowed things down and focused on rebuilding my strength, muscle by muscle. It took some time, but I got there.

> **The biggest advantage of returning to training was that it cleared my mind. I was able to escape from a world of nappies and piles of washing to be outside, breathing the fresh air.**

This awakened my mind and gave me a better understanding of what my body needed in order to move forwards. Some days I would run with the pram; others I would just do a fast walk, but either way, I made sure that cardio was part of my day. Taking one small step at a time, I gradually found my way back to myself.

Understanding hormones

What happens to our hormones after having a baby? The truth is, many women don't know. My university studies and love of kids did not prepare me for the hormonal changes I experienced after giving birth, even though I thought I knew what I was in for.

After childbirth, you get a glimpse into the future and it is not so appealing. The hormonal changes following pregnancy begin very quickly after the delivery of the baby and, more importantly, the placenta. During pregnancy, oestrogen levels are very high, which is one of the causes of nausea and sickness in early pregnancy. The delivery of the placenta triggers a sudden and severe drop in oestrogen and progesterone levels, making women experience hormonal changes similar to menopause. These range from hot flushes and thinning hair to dry skin. The loss of oestrogen causes tissues to become thin, delicate and sensitive. Hormonal changes can also affect women mentally, making them more inclined to experience a low mood. The good news is that this is temporary. Personally, I struggled to get out of my own hole.

Birth can make our periods go a little haywire, too. Women who have had very light periods before pregnancy often find their periods are much heavier after giving birth. If they are particularly bad, an endocrinologist, or hormone specialist, can help with various treatment options.

The most important thing to know about our hormones is that pregnancy, childbirth and being a mother—no matter how big your children get—is hard work on our bodies. If you want to have healthy hormones for bone strength, cardiovascular health and general wellbeing, you must put some energy into caring for yourself. Many mums are mentally and physically exhausted, with high stress levels, low iron and poor sleep. They struggle with premenstrual tension and continue to gain or lose too much weight.

The best piece of advice I can give you is to spend at least some of your precious time looking after yourself: eat that piece of fruit, take that yoga class, spend an hour reading a book or treat yourself to a massage. Your body (and mind) will thank you for it.

Hyperthyroidism

Research states that up to one in ten women's thyroid glands will stop working correctly in the months after giving birth. (The main hormone made by our thyroid gland is thyroxin, which is released into the bloodstream and is crucial for digestion, muscle function and energy levels, among other things.) This usually causes a short phase of hyperthyroidism, or overactive thyroid, in the first few months after birth.

Hyperthyroidism makes us feel slightly hyperactive and makes weight loss easy, which may sound like an attractive prospect to many of us mums, but it's a bit like having too many coffees after a long night: it is not a pleasant source of energy. Those women unlucky enough to suffer the opposite condition—hypothyroidism—experience tiredness, weight gain, feeling cold, heavy periods and thinning hair. Thankfully, both hyperthyroidism and hypothyroidism are usually brief and treatable conditions. If your symptoms persist, always consult a doctor.

Negative self-talk

Having children changed my entire outlook on life. I suddenly felt the pain of other people more closely. I felt affected by victims of crime, war and drug addiction, and noticed how much mothers suffered from these tragic events.

Motherhood is a mind-expanding form of love.

It teaches us selflessness, patience and forgiveness. We learn to love in an unconditional way and become less judgmental of others. Of course, there are times when we resent our children. I admit I've had these feelings, especially through both pregnancies and births. Now, I have a sense of overwhelming love for them and a deep desire to protect them.

After I had my children, I realised that all my previous loves had been selfish; I had been constantly thinking about myself. This was a huge part of my struggle after having children. Even as I write about this painful part of my life, all the feelings of incompetence resurface. I struggled to be a mum at first because I was so caught up in myself. Many days I would cry, angry with myself for being so bad at it. I would ask myself, 'Why can't I get this baby to sleep?', 'Why was my pregnancy so bad?', 'Why does my child cry all day and night?'

Everyone kept saying, 'Isn't this a beautiful time of your life?' and I would think, 'Are you kidding?' I was trapped in a nonstop nappy-changing, constant-feeding hell with no sleep and no relief. Every morning, I woke up to the monotony of washing, cleaning, poo. I was utterly depressed. I felt like I was not important as an individual anymore, only as a mother. It was all about the baby.

What I needed was to find a way out of my own mind. All that negative self-talk was causing my issues, but I didn't realise it at the time. This is unbelievably common for new mothers as they morph into a new identity. I had thought birth was bad, but this remaking of myself had no end in sight.

Gradually, I began to notice my tendency to generalise my negativity. Too often, I would extrapolate one negative thing to make everything dreadful. I was catastrophising and playing the 'Blame Game'. Slowly, I found ways to turn this around. I busied myself finding gratitude in small wins. For example, if I got time to go for a walk, I would congratulate myself. In my former life as a triathlete, I had gotten so used to grand accolades that little wins didn't seem worthy. Unravelling this and finding joy in small pleasures challenged my negative self-talk and allowed me to repurpose it into something helpful.

Looking back, life really wasn't that bad. Of course, hormones played their part, but it would have been so much easier if I had consciously focused on the good in my life the way I do now. I would have appreciated the time that I had to nurture my first-born child. I believe that many of my issues came about because I was in such a rush to get my pre-baby life back rather than enjoying my new one. It was unrealistic; nothing is the same after you've had a child.

Some of the notes I took in the first few months after giving birth were quite disturbing, but the act of writing them down helped immensely to soothe my negative self-talk. When my baby was crying and crying and crying, when my frustrations and helplessness overcame me, this was the only way to unleash my emotions without causing damage or hurt. I would recommend this as a tool to any new mother in need of an outlet.

Find gratitude in small wins ☆

Isolation and postnatal depression

Before becoming a mother, I was sure that I could do it—and do it well. It would all be so easy. After all, I had watched and cared for children in my classroom for years. I love kids.

I was in for a rude shock. As new mothers will tell you, we are all too often on our own. This was certainly not what I was used to. In Western culture, mothering often creates physical isolation from other adults. Our days and nights are focused on caring for the baby, and we tend to their needs before our own.

Often, we have very few people to turn to when we need support the most. In my pre-baby life of working, studying and being an athlete, I had a community of people around me, including my wonderful girlfriends, with whom I could discuss day-to-day grievances and joke about life. But, as a mother, I was home alone with my child for most of the day, every day. In the early weeks, the amount of time I spent with adults declined rapidly. Old friends and family were busy with their lives. Some people were terrified of babies and stayed away. I quickly fell into a state of postnatal depression.

To make matters worse, my new-found existence ran on a set schedule. Feeding, sleeping and nappy changing happened at certain times. It took longer to get places and, when I did arrive, I was often exhausted and covered in baby vomit. My brain couldn't keep up with conversations and my body didn't look like it used to. Yet, I seemed to be surrounded by other parents or people who totally had it together: their babies were sleeping well and everything was great. I'd try to discuss my problems only to find that the other person just talked about themselves, gave unwelcome or unhelpful advice, or changed the subject entirely. I felt unheard and, worse, judged. Of course, many of my friends were great allies and helped me sort out my problems, but those who didn't have children often found it hard to understand the changes in my life. It was a lonely, difficult time.

Some mums are lucky to have a dependable person to speak to, whether a mother, partner or a friend. But even if you have the most amazing person to listen to your problems, sometimes those problems are overwhelming for them, too.

My son was a reflux baby: he vomited all the time and could not be still. He struggled to sleep most nights, and settling him was a challenge when the burning sensation was hurting his poor little throat. I tried everything. I was breastfeeding and allowing him to nuzzle continuously, which helped him but was exhausting for me. I was intensely sleep deprived, living on fast sugars and carbs just to stay awake. (In retrospect, this was probably causing a lot of his issues, but I did not know then what I know now about food and its effect on the breastmilk we feed our babies.) My little man screamed a lot. This caused me a lot of anxiety, which then caused him anxiety, which caused more reflux. It was a vicious circle and I did not know how to break it.

Motherhood forces women into a new kind of self-sufficiency. We have to serve the needs of others, but we must also find a way to nourish and love ourselves.

Acknowledge that you need and deserve time to take care of yourself; it is the only way we can go the distance.

The only way I coped was by drawing on my inner resources and balancing myself.

It is rare that postnatal depression can be cured by self-sufficiency alone, and many women find it helpful to seek professional support. We might want to do it all ourselves, but it is not necessary to suffer alone in silence. A qualified psychologist or counsellor can help you find your way through the maze and give you practical tools and strategies to overcome your depression. Always seek the advice of your primary healthcare professional if you are feeling overwhelmed.

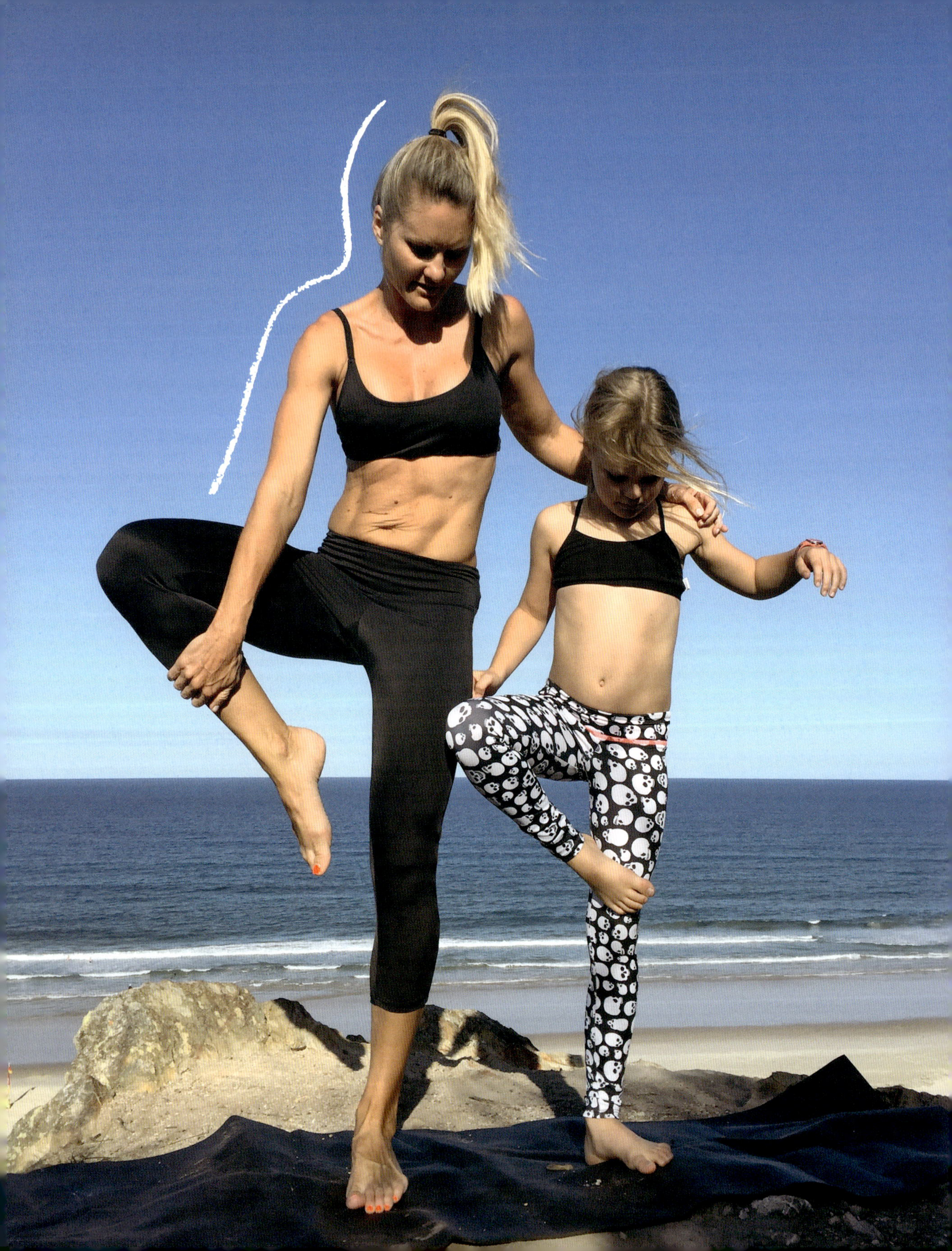

A raw deal

In most two-parent households, both parents are stretched by the demands of modern family life, but it is, overwhelmingly, the mother who receives the shabby end of the deal. Conditions have improved since our parents' generation, but how much better is it really? Women are still saddled with all sorts of responsibilities, from the needs of their children to the needs of their partners in the home, kitchen—and bedroom. A mother must keep everyone happy, everywhere, all the time and then still find time for herself.

Let's be honest: we women set our own bars pretty high, so it's no surprise that we feel like we've let ourselves—and everyone else—down when we don't reach them. We try to be Wonder Woman, proving that we can have it all, but this is often where we fall down. In this book, I want to share my truth, and I want to help you find yours, too.

I have decided that the only answer is to do the best we can in our unique situations and be happy with that. No two lives are the same. The most important thing is that we stop judging other women and the choices they make for themselves and their families.

One day at the gym, I overheard two women on the treadmills next to me. They were discussing a mutual friend who had paid for a cleaner to help her get organised. The women were saying how unfair this was, questioning why she wasn't doing it herself. I believe such jealousy and righteousness are uncalled for. There is nothing wrong with utilising other people for help.

Think of it this way: what this woman did provided another person with a job, enabled her to spend more quality time with her child, and generally took some pressure off. It's a win-win situation.

After all the years of feminist struggle by bold, heroic women all over the world, it's truly upsetting to see women tearing each other down. Instead, we should redirect our energy into building each other up.

Women often try to be Wonder Woman

Mum guilt

I believe we mothers never live a day without guilt or worrying about something, even if it's something small. We worry about whether we have enough time, or whether we gave enough energy to a particular event or person. Of course, our greatest feelings of guilt are over our children: do they have everything they need? Should we be spending time with them instead of doing chores? We put so much pressure on ourselves to be the perfect mother. We feel like failures if we can't do everything exactly right.

Guilt is such a confusing emotion. It undermines our happiness. We must treat guilt like we treat all other mind games: notice when it crops up, accept the feelings that arise, look at the causes and note the effects on our bodies. When you identify all these things, notice whether they are helpful or not. Guilt can be a great prompt to improve some aspects of our lives but, more often, we simply turn all those guilty feelings into a kind of anti-mantra and use it to make ourselves miserable. Notice this, stop, and remind yourself that you are not Wonder Woman—and that no one asked you to be.

> *It is okay not to complete everything and not to do everything perfectly.*

It's important to move past this feeling quickly. I managed to do this by writing and becoming conscious of my feelings.

Choosing happiness

We all face challenges along the way that can drastically change the course of our lives, but it is how we deal with these problems that matters most. Becoming a single mum was hard. The simplest of tasks became difficult, and trying to keep up with the demands of my children, my household and my job felt impossible. Everything was down to me, from the cleaning and laundry to DIY jobs and dropping the kids off at after-school activities.

Slowly, I managed to sort out my head and my heart, and regained my equilibrium. It took a long time, but this is how the beautiful chaos of the life I have today was born. I had to realise I could access the sense of hope and love I was searching for, right under the roof I provided. It was right there in my arms and in my love for my children. I stopped beating myself up for trying to manage it all and failing. I drafted my children as my teammates and allocated jobs and chores so everyone could pitch in to the running of the household. Pretty soon, I came to see that not only could we survive this way, but thrive, too. And, suddenly, being single didn't seem so bad.

We all face the challenge of being happy. In the face of this challenge, we tend to do one of two things: 1) get on with the business of celebrating the life we have, or 2) spend our time feeling miserable and wishing it was different.

I now celebrate being single. For many years, I yearned for a new marriage, but my path was laid in another direction. Perhaps, deep down, I also yearned for freedom.

Whenever we wish or demand things to be different, we suffer emotionally. The harder we wish, the more we suffer. Conversely, the more we embrace what is, rather than what could be, the more content we become. Contentment breeds more contentment.

Being single is no better or worse than being married. It is merely a different set of circumstances, complete with different advantages and disadvantages. The mistake so many people make—whether

Treat your children like your teammates and they will step up

Becoming a mum 25

single or married—is that they focus on the disadvantages and fail to celebrate the good stuff. I know for a fact that it's entirely possible to learn to celebrate the life you have, no matter what your circumstances. And, once the attitude of celebration enters the picture, you're on your way to the life of your dreams.

No matter what adversity you have faced, you can become more productive, more positive and see the love in every aspect of life. You can challenge your attitude and thoughts to become helpful and honest with everyone around you, value all the experiences you have, and see mistakes as opportunities to learn rather than failures. I would love to see a change in the way women feel, and to give them the strength to make a stand for the lives they really want.

Focusing on inner beauty

Have you ever looked at someone and noticed how lively and dynamic they are? How much energy and light radiates from them? Not because they are outstandingly beautiful, but because they have a certain magnetism? This kind of energy comes from within, and the only way to cultivate it is to be honest and true to yourself. Once you have grown to understand who you really are, you can achieve a balance between mind, body and spirit. No matter what your physical characteristics, when you are genuinely happy and connected to your spirit, you light up from within.

It is easy to lose sight of our inner beauty when we're focused on achieving external beauty. After becoming mothers, most women feel pressured to get back in shape as soon as possible. (I certainly did.) But pause to remember this: you have just undergone a complete metamorphosis. You are getting to know a new side of yourself, which is both wondrous and frightening. Give yourself permission to slow down and discover this new person and the joy and light that radiates from within. You will lose those 'new mum' kilos in time, but this precious period with your newbown is fleeting.

BE IN LOVE

WITH YOUR LIFE

Every single second of it

Nurturing enthusiasm

It's not difficult to see why new mothers struggle to be enthusiastic—about anything, really. They're exhausted, frazzled and hormonal, and possibly suffering from postnatal depression. And, even though they are filled with love for their newborns, finding the energy to be enthusiastic seems impossible. However, showing enthusiasm, no matter how counterintuitive it feels, might actually improve your energy.

When we allow enthusiasm to bubble up, we are able to share an abundance of joy with others. This energy is magnetic and contagious, and is the easiest way to make yourself and others feel instantly better. It improves confidence, lifts mood and shows those around you that, despite the trials of motherhood, you are there for your friends and family.

I am genuinely interested in everyone I meet. I always hope that I can learn something new from them. Some people find this kind of enthusiasm overbearing or even annoying or fake, but I just can't help it. Ever since I began focusing on gratitude and positivity, I have been constantly interested in the world around me and bubbling with joy. As you express your enthusiasm for life, people will be more inclined to open up and share their dreams and aspirations, and it feels good when others trust you and feel supported.

FINDING THE 'GREAT' IN GRATEFUL

All too often we allow the feeling of being overwhelmed and our desire for achievement and material satisfaction to overshadow the most precious things in our lives, such as our health, our family and our friends. In our race to enjoy the highest highs, we tend to miss the small and simple pleasures, which are generally the most memorable.

The hormonal highs and lows of motherhood can be brutal, but it's important to recognise that, largely, these emotional shifts are due to a lack of sleep and the general chaos of those challenging early days of motherhood. While worrying about nappy changing, sleeping routines and endless piles of washing, we may lose sight of the big picture. We need to get better at stopping, even just for five short minutes, and being present in what is actually important.

When we feel overwhelmed, we have a tendency to focus on what is wrong, irritating or missing, rather than what is beautiful and special. Our focus is on looking for problems, which only makes problems seem bigger. Unfortunately, this type of attention feeds on itself and quickly becomes a way of thinking. We end up framing everything in a negative light and expecting things to go wrong. But, when we turn our attention to what is going well in our lives, what is successful and enriching, we undergo a magical transformation: the more you look for the good, the more the good sees you. The more you look for happiness, the more it finds you.

To get back in touch with the things you are grateful for, visualise a deck of cards. Imagine all the cards laid out in front of you. On one side they say 'sad' and on the other, 'happy'. Imagine that all the cards have the 'happy' side facing up. Now, think about your day and everything that has happened. (You can ask your children to talk about theirs, too.) Every time your thoughts begin leading to a negative place, think of the 'happy' side of the card: what was good and positive about the situation? What can you learn from it? While we need to acknowledge the 'sad' sides of the cards to process the events, remember that there is another 'happy' side to that same card. Some people get so good at this mindfulness technique that they can utilise it to overcome feelings of angst and irritation in just about any setting. This does not mean that you need to pretend things are awesome all the time, or that you should ignore the pain and ugliness in the world. But noticing beauty first and being honest and reflective can redirect your energy and focus onto the things that matter.

Celebrating the big stuff provides fleeting moments of happiness. However, if you feel grateful for the small things, too, you will be happy the majority of the time, because simple, heartwarming pleasures are everywhere we look.

2

Plan your new life

PRACTICAL TIPS TO MAKE IT WORK

Finding a healthy balance between work, children, family and friends as a new mum can be an arduous task. There is so much to fit in and, generally, never enough time to do it all. Whether you have a full-time career, do part-time work or are a stay-at-home mum, every role requires a juggling act. In order to find a healthy balance, you must involve the whole family and be prepared to share the workload.

Most women are no longer the 'housewives' that our parents'—and grandparents'—generations once knew. We have careers, goals, dreams and needs, in addition to raising our children. Why then do so many women still put their needs last, ensuring the family stays on track and not allowing any personal time for rest and recuperation? If your answer is: 'If I don't do it, no one else will,' then rest assured, you're not alone. But you needn't do it all yourself.

> **By introducing some practical changes for the whole family, you can free up time and teach your children valuable life skills in the process.**

Working out what needed to be done, when, where, by whom and so on, for every person in the family, was one of the most important steps I took towards getting my life—and my family's life—back into balance. As well as setting goals for the future, planning what was happening on a weekly basis really got me to where I am today. Now, scheduling and goal-setting are integral parts of my daily life, and I owe so much of my success (at home and at work) to the practical strategies in this chapter.

Scheduling

Without a doubt, one of the biggest causes of stress for most people is the daily rush to fit in too many things. We tend to deny the reality of how long it takes to complete certain tasks and end up overcommitting ourselves. This, in turn, makes us feel like failures and leads to untold anxiety and stress.

One of the first rules of scheduling is to not bite off more than you can realistically chew. This looks different for everyone, so make a plan and only attempt what you know you can manage in a single day. You will end it feeling accomplished and organised instead of stressed and guilty.

FACTOR IN DELAYS

A second common scheduling mistake is not allowing time for delays. Your commute to work is usually only 30 minutes, but by the time your child loses a shoe or a drink bottle, or you can't find your car keys, the schedule quickly unravels and you find yourself running 15 minutes late—to everything. This is when the stress sets in and continues throughout the day, making you feel frazzled, exhausted and incapable. You start to wonder why everyone else seems to have it together and you don't.

It might seem obvious, but leaving more time than you need takes an enormous amount of pressure off. Instead of rushing around, you feel calm and secure. You spend less time apologising to colleagues, and less time yelling at the kids for making you late (which is a bit unfair, considering it was your fault for trying to fit too much in). It's a preventative measure that will encourage you to schedule fewer things so you don't become overwhelmed.

Factor in an extra 15 minutes

SET PRIORITIES

When you rush, trying to fit everything in, it's nearly impossible to enjoy the process. What could be a fun car ride to school quickly descends into a frustrated argument—and one that you will inevitably feel guilty about later. Try scheduling your day around what is going to make you happy and allowing enough time for those things first. For example, if it's important to you to walk your kids to school, get up half an hour earlier and make sure you have the time. That way, you can be in the present and enjoy the journey instead of wishing it away as you rush to the next task.

CREATE A FAMILY SCHEDULE

Planning a family schedule involves communication and the complete understanding—and willingness—of everyone in the house. Children love having a sense of purpose and accomplishment, and assigning them simple chores helps them to realise their role in the family. A family schedule is also a great way to teach them responsibility as it builds accountability into their daily lives.

When I prepare my family schedule (see opposite), I write down all the weekly tasks, and I mean everything. It starts with a family discussion about the upcoming week: what we need to factor in and who has what planned. By involving everyone in the schedule, it becomes a responsibility that we all contribute to. I set it up as a roster system. Everyone living in the house must help and it has to be a team effort, otherwise it will not work.

It might sound silly, but we even schedule time to do the schedule. It's usually on a Sunday evening over dinner. We discuss what each person needs to get done that week in addition to the usual weekly chores, and we look at how we can help each other achieve it. Make sure your family helps you achieve your goals, too, even if it's just getting a nice long soak in the bath.

Family schedule

- ☐ Laundry
- ☐ Cleaning
- ☐ Gardening
- ☐ Exercise
- ☐ Food prep (meal-planning, prep and cooking)
- ☐ Training/sport
- ☐ Kids' term dates, homework, assignments, assemblies and extracurricular activities
- ☐ Grocery shopping
- ☐ Petrol
- ☐ Personal admin (paying bills, answering emails, going to the post office)
- ☐ Personal grooming (haircuts, facial, pedicure, waxing, a long soak in the bath—you name it, it's on the list)
- ☐ Health (doctor, chiropractor, physiotherapist, massage and so on)
- ☐ Other weekly errands (such as visiting your mother-in-law)
- ☐ Big family goals (from experiences to large purchases)

Children and chores

Chores are key to children's development. Not only do they teach children to value and care for their own possessions, but they learn to take pride in the home they live in, too. Just like teaching manners, chores are part of learning respect. Children who have self-respect are happier and find life—and interactions with others—easier to deal with.

Chores prepare a child for living well. As all adults understand, life is no picnic and, these days, many children are allowed to simply sit around without partaking in household chores. As much as you might want to pamper your children, it actually does them a disservice to encourage this kind of behaviour. We devalue them and end up raising lazy, privileged children, teens and young adults with little respect for themselves and for others.

HERE ARE A FEW TIPS FOR SETTING CHORES:

- Set chores from an early age.
- Create a chores list and put it somewhere prominent in the house.
- Make sure the chores are distributed evenly to avoid arguments, and rotate them regularly so that everyone does a bit of everything.
- Be tough on teens: remove devices immediately if chores have not been completed. As hard as it might feel, you must be tough to teach them to take responsibility for their own lives.
- Make the list of chores as visible as possible—either give out personal lists or create a family schedule board.

Chores teach children that life is not always a picnic

HOUSEHOLD CHORES

Having a checklist of household chores for all age categories is a good way to make sure your children gradually build up to doing them and aren't afraid to tackle new things.

I suggest starting at age four with a single simple chore, then adding one chore each year until the child is 16 years old, creating a weekly list of thirteen chores. Each chore should be gender-neutral to ensure that all children understand that they have the same capabilities and responsibilities around the home. Here are some ideas:

Perfect chores for kids

AGE 4: Place personal clothing in the washing basket.

AGE 5: Water the plants.

AGE 6: Make own bed/replace the bedsheets.

AGE 7: Clear the dinner table.

AGE 8: Change the rubbish bin liner.

AGE 9: Vacuum and mop the floors.

AGE 10: Clean the toilets/shower screen.

AGE 11: Pack and unpack the dishwasher/do the washing up.

AGE 12: Clean the windows/hang out the clothes.

AGE 13: Cook a meal.

AGE 14: Mow the grass/help with the weeding.

AGE 15: Complete the washing and folding/ironing.

AGE 16: Wash and vacuum the car.

Reinforce good behaviour by showing respect

PERSONAL CHORES

BRUSH HAIR.
Girls can learn to do their own ponytails by the age of nine.

BRUSH TEETH.

TIDY ROOM.
Make sure you show them what it looks like when it's clean first so they understand what is expected.

GET DRESSED.

TIE SHOELACES.

USE A KNIFE AND FORK.

WRITE A SHORT NOTE/MAKE A LIST.

Personal chores—meaning, responsibilities around personal hygiene and caring for your own things—can be taught from as young as five. Here are some examples:

HOW TO ENCOURAGE CHORES

Chores are a part of life, not something to do for a reward. Demonstrate this to your children by explaining that Mum doesn't get a reward every time she picks up a towel from the bathroom floor, and Dad doesn't get a reward every time he takes the rubbish out. Remind children that completing chores is a show of respect for the home they live in, both for themselves and for their parents.

That said, it's important to reinforce good behaviour by showing your appreciation and pride for every chore your child completes.

FOR EXAMPLE:

- Use positive reinforcement by saying what a great job they have done, even if it's not exactly right.
- Show them how to do the chore properly, then repeat the chore as a team before allowing them to complete it alone.
- Play a game afterwards as a reward rather than using money or food as enticement. Never use food to reward any kind of behaviour, as this encourages children to associate food with gratification. Instead, the pleasure should be in the fulfilment of having completed the task.

And remember: you are not being harsh by expecting your children to do chores. You are teaching them life skills. If you're still in any doubt, think of it like this: if a child can use a device, such as an iPhone, computer or tablet, then they can certainly complete some simple chores.

Plan your new life 39

Priorities and goals

Are you getting caught up in what others want you to do? I am not talking about your kids or your partner, but your wider circle of friends, extended family or even strangers on the internet. Too often, we let other people set our goals for us, whether it's a well-meaning friend insisting that you go to yoga with her, a mother-in-law making 'helpful' suggestions for how to raise your kids, or a school wanting you to get involved in a sports team. It is easy to allow ourselves—and our lives—to be led by other people, but only you can know what your priorities should be.

The habit of 'keeping up with the Joneses' is still alive and well. We worry too much about what others think. It is common for mothers to fear that their kids may be left out if they are not doing the same extracurricular activities as everyone else. If we are really honest with ourselves though, we are the ones signing our kids up to the endless sports teams, sleepovers and school plays. These are *our* priorities, not theirs. And all we end up teaching them is the habit of rushing from place to place. Worse, we are at risk of putting our children under pressure to be something that they are not.

Similarly, we need to stop wearing the word 'busy' like a badge of honour. Busy is a trap. It's making us sick. The energy involved in being constantly busy is exhausting and regularly at odds with how we would truly like to be living.

> **Focus on living an authentic life according to your values, not the values of fellow school mums and work colleagues.**

Something I find helpful is to set my priorities and then regularly reassess them: are they realistic? Are they making me and my family happy? If they're not, I ditch them.

GOAL-SETTING

When we set simple daily goals and actually achieve them, we gain confidence and assurance that we can tackle anything.

I set daily, weekly, monthly and yearly goals, and I also set life goals, writing them in a diary on my bedside table and altering them all the time. The physical act of writing them down and visualising them makes my goals feel more achievable. It's a show of commitment to myself, and I'm more likely to reach them because I have recorded them. I want you to try it: write down the goals you have right now. It might be getting to the next chapter of this book so you can go to sleep, or it might be putting away that pile of clothes.

Next, write down your goals for the week. They can be as simple as drink more water, eat more broccoli or switch off technology earlier in the evening.

Now, write down the coming month's goals. These might include a weekend away or a mountain walk. It might be to complete your new fitness program without cheating, or something larger, like finishing landscaping your garden. Whatever you want, write it down, no matter how impossible it seems right now.

Do the same with your goals for the year. Maybe you want to get healthy or go on a holiday. Write it down in detail.

Visualise it all and pretend to be there: smell it and touch it. I like to put these big, whole-family, long-term goals up on the family schedule board (see page 36) so everyone can see them and be reminded of them. It helps everyone pull together to work towards the collective goal.

Check back weekly and monthly on your goals, and I bet you achieve more than 50 per cent of them. The slightest shift in your intention, or in changing your attitude, will turn amazing possibilities into reality.

A shift in your intention will turn possibilities into reality

Plan your new life

Avoiding time-wasters

All of your planning and scheduling will be for nothing if you fall into the trap of the biggest time-wasters: smart phones and social media. Step away from the scroll. Force yourself to check your apps only once or twice a day and then put your phone away where you can't see it. Allocate 'social media time' in the morning and evening, and try to cap it at 15 minutes. There are even apps and programs that can help you do this by restricting your browser access to certain websites.

> *Social media is addictive, but empty. Make sure your life stays full.*

Time is the most valuable asset we have, yet we waste so much of it. And identifying time that we can save is often just as hard. Are you getting up too late? What about going to bed too early? What do you do when you first come in from work? That period between coming in and cooking dinner is a valuable window, but often we feel too tired or disinclined to use it. If we manage our time properly, we will be able to fit more into our day and gain a sense of peace and accomplishment.

42 Fit Mama

Three ways to fit more into your day

There are times when you don't have a choice but to pack a lot into your day. Want to make it as stress-free as possible? Here are some tips:

1 USE A TIMER. This might sound extreme, but it's helpful for some, even most, tasks in a given day. Instead of looking at your day like a swamp of a million things you have to wade through to reach the other side, try to tackle it bit by bit. Choose a time—say, 25 minutes—and set the timer. When the timer goes off, take a five-minute break, then reset it and start the next task. I personally find that this technique helps me focus on the job at hand and get it done efficiently instead of meandering through it. It's especially good for pre- and post-school tasks, such as preparing lunchboxes, putting washing on, folding laundry or doing a workout.

A few more tips for maximising your timed tasks include: switch off the TV to avoid distraction, turn off your phone or set it to silent mode, and write a list of tasks in the order you want to complete them and don't deviate from the list.

2 MINIMISE DECISIONS. The easiest way to remove some decision-making from my day is to embrace repetition. I tend to cook the same meals most weeks, with a few exceptions when we want to try something new or need a treat. I'm familiar with the recipes and don't need to spend time looking them up. It also helps when I come to write the shopping list; I know exactly what I need each week.

The same goes for what I wear. During the week, I tend to stick to the same half a dozen items that I know suit me well and are comfortable and easy to wash and wear. I don't have time to spend 15 minutes every morning staring blankly at my wardrobe, and I'm sure you don't either. This also makes wearing different clothes at the weekend more enjoyable, especially when you get to dress up a bit.

3 GET UP EARLIER. Don't whine, just do it. It is about gaining an extra 30 minutes to spend on yourself and your goals without the demands of others. That extra half an hour every morning, while everyone else is still asleep or stirring, is my time to get organised and get on top of a few chores before the chaos starts.

Plan your new life 43

3

Find your strength

THE ABC OF GETTING FIT

Many women don't know how to go about getting rid of their mum bods. Should they focus on cardio instead of weights? Or stick to low-impact exercises? What about high-intensity interval training (HIIT)? It's a bit of a minefield.

After high school, I obtained a Certificate in Personal Training, which gave me all the tools I needed to build a successful and sustainable fitness routine. Over my many years of training for competitions, I used a lot of gyms and felt very comfortable in them. I worked out how to get exactly the results I was after. But, for the average mum, it's not that straightforward.

I recommend starting with sound information, and the best way to get this is from a qualified personal trainer. Instead of winging it in the gym—and risking injury—trainers can teach you good technique and etiquette, and build a program around your specific needs and goals. They can also help you get motivated to start and maintain your routine, which is essential to success.

Getting motivated

Distil what it is you really want

Motivation. It eludes many of us, but we can't get much done without it. Distilling what it is you really want and using it to motivate yourself is the first step towards achieving your goals. Do you want to lose weight? Tone up? Be more mobile for your children? While it's important to determine these macro goals, we have to drill down even further and look at the detailed work they will entail.

Mapping out the detailed changes you have to make and the techniques you will use to reach your goal is the only way to make it happen. For example, I sought to better my overall health. I didn't want to sneeze all the time. I didn't want to suffer through constant hayfever, itchy eyes and asthma. So I set to work gathering as much information as possible about how I could turn it around. I used this knowledge to plan a new health regime and created a fitness plan that suited where I was in my process, and one that could be tweaked and developed as my health and strength improved.

Ways to kickstart your motivation

WORK OUT WITH FRIENDS. When we turn our training into something social by involving friends, it gives us more motivation to show up. It also makes us more accountable, as we are less likely to let our friends down.

TRY A NEW FITNESS CLASS or a new venue to keep things fresh.

GET SWEATY. Sweating clears your pores and helps detoxify your body, making you feel great. Aim to get as sweaty as possible, and add a steam at the end of the session to really invigorate yourself.

LISTEN TO MUSIC WITH PUMPING, LOUD BASS. The constant beat helps you to stay focused and keep time. Try training with headphones when you are alone. It helps the brain switch off to external sounds and puts you in a calm, relaxed state.

HAVE A TRAINING PLAN. Know what you are going to do before you begin. Write down your session or follow a tailored fitness program and promise yourself that you will see it through to the end.

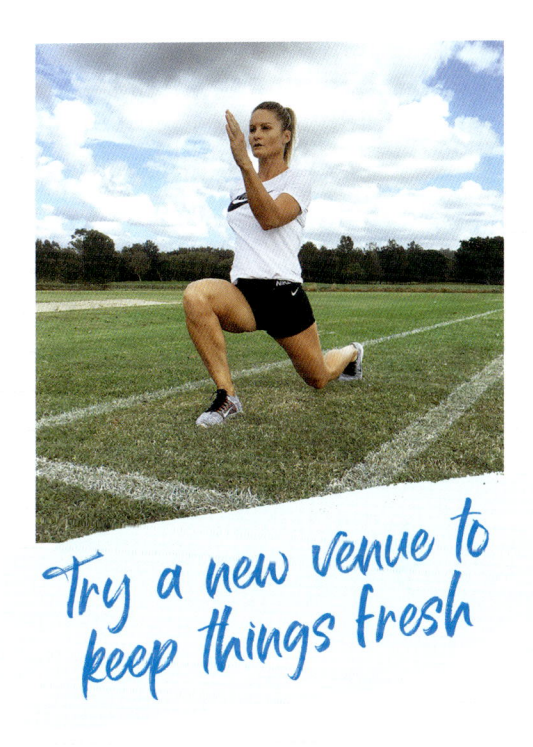

Try a new venue to keep things fresh

DON'T TELL YOURSELF YOU'RE TOO TIRED TO TRAIN. Chances are you're going to be at least a little tired most of the time (especially if you have kids), so don't let it become a barrier to working out. Work through the tiredness and find your motivation. You'll thank yourself at the end of the session.

EMBRACE THE HUMBLE WALK. Walk for 30 minutes every morning, before work and school, or in the evening, rather than sitting in front of the TV or glued to technology. If you walk as a family, everyone can reap the health benefits and it makes a great time for catching up on the day.

Find your strength

Cardio training

'Cardio' is any activity that stimulates your body and increases blood flow through your cardiovascular system. It is a continuous exercise that directly impacts your endurance and strength, and it's an essential element of a good fitness routine.

Complete a cardiovascular (raised heart rate) activity every day, without fail. This could include a fast walk, a run, cycle or a mini functional-fitness circuit. Aim for 30 minutes every day before breakfast. 'Fasted cardio', or doing a cardio workout before you eat, is the most effective method of cardio as it supercharges your system and breaks down fat cells. Take the kids on bikes or scooters and run alongside them—whatever works for you, but just make sure you do it.

I get up, get dressed and then head out to do 30–40 minutes of nonstop cardio first thing in the morning every single day.

TRAINING AROUND YOUR MENSTRUAL CYCLE

A woman's menstrual cycle has a huge impact on her ability to exercise. It affects mood, energy levels and physical strength. How hard we can work out and how quickly we recover fluctuates drastically throughout the month. About two weeks before your period, fluid levels and body temperature rise, making you prone to overheating. Around the time of ovulation, your ligaments loosen, making it easier to strain yourself, as your ligaments are at their most elastic. Immediately before your period, fatigue and clumsiness can take a hold, not to mention irritability and emotion. During this most delicate phase, try to scale things back a little. Instead of high-intensity exercise, try longer walks, lighter weights and easy abdominal workouts. I like to think of my period as a powerful shedding and renewal; it's a time to release all the feelings I had bottled up the previous month.

The best cardio activities for women

INDOOR

Skipping
+
Stationary cycling/ RPM/spinning
+
Treadmill running/ walking
+
Martial arts
+
Cross-training

OUTDOOR

Skipping
+
Cycling
+
Walking
+
Running
+
Boxing

Other types of training

Cardiovascular training alone will not give you the best body shape. It will help you to lose weight and maintain a healthy weight, and it is absolutely necessary for fitness and mobility, but it's not the only piece of the puzzle. If you really want to sculpt your body, you will need to incorporate other forms of exercise.

They say variety is the spice of life, and that's certainly true for fitness training. The more you mix it up, the more you keep your body guessing and the faster you will see results. Just as you get tired and bored with the same old routine, so does your body, and the longer you carry on repeating the same moves, the less your body will respond. It's also a motivation killer. Keep yourself engaged by changing up what you do every couple of weeks.

I do a mixture of weight circuits, spin/RPM classes, cardio, outdoor cycling, swimming (including ocean swimming), skateboarding and yoga every single week. I also walk or run every day.

INTERVAL TRAINING

Interval training is the most successful way to keep in shape. This means altering your speed and intensity throughout the training session. It is proven to burn more calories in a shorter period of time, which is a bonus for busy working mums. Aim for 10 seconds on, 30 seconds off, then build from there, slowly increasing the amount of work time and decreasing your rest period. It will force you to prioritise quality over quantity.

> *If you are able to scroll on your phone while walking on the treadmill, you are not working hard enough.*

STRENGTH TRAINING

Weight training for women is the key to health, longevity and overall wellness. I can't emphasise enough how important it is. A well-balanced strength program, with high repetitions and varied weights, creates lean muscle and a taut, feminine body shape.

Resistance training, whether using weights or bands, places weighted stress on the muscles, forcing them to grow and strengthen. As they grow, they increase in size, resulting in a taut, defined and smooth-looking body shape.

Weight training creates a much greater (and longer) calorie burn than cardio training.

This is because lean muscle requires more energy to maintain itself than fat. Therefore, the more muscle you have, the more calories you need (and burn) each day.

While we're talking about weight training, let me dispel a popular myth: lifting weights will not make you bulky or masculine-looking. Women are physiologically different to men and, while you do see the occasional female bodybuilder with freakishly large muscles, this is not the norm; most women can't achieve this physique even after years of weight training.

So, instead of worrying about looking bulky, focus on following a strength program designed for women. This is very important, as male-specific weight programs are counterproductive for women and don't target the areas necessary to create a beautiful female physique, so don't be tempted to follow your husband's or boyfriend's program. Lifting too-heavy weights can also cause significant injury, so leave those 20 kg dumbbells on the rack.

Weight training to retain muscle mass becomes even more important as we age

Find your strength 51

SPEED WEIGHT CIRCUITS

Speed weight circuits are workouts that are completed as quickly as possible while maintaining good stability and alignment. A timer will help you stay on track during these sessions, and a good gym instructor or personal trainer can ensure you use the right technique.

Aim to complete speed weight circuits three times per week with a two-minute run or cycle in between each set.

Strength training with fast repetitions is great for building lean muscle, but make sure you aren't overdoing it with heavy weights. Women should never lift more than their body weight. Lifting heavy weights has a detrimental effect on the body, causing the muscles to shorten and become inflexible. Make sure you do not exceed 10 kg for your upper body and 70 kg for your lower body. (This is what I personally use.)

Always ensure you are well aligned, especially when moving at speed, and never, ever drop the weights. Instead, aim for slow, controlled movements at all times to reduce the likelihood of injury and to challenge your body. Better yet, aim to move even more slowly on the way down than you did on the way up, which will create longer, leaner muscle. If you feel the need to drop the weights, try to put them down quickly instead of dropping them from a height, which can put excess strain on your body, not to mention startle those working out around you.

If you want to attempt a heavy-weight session to build strength in your muscle fibres, always enlist the help of a gym instructor or friend to spot you. Ensure that you have a good grip on the weights, that your feet are firmly and evenly planted, and that you are using good technique. Aim to complete any heavier sets in the middle of your workout—after you have warmed up, but before the end of the session muscle fatigue has set in.

Combining light weights with speed training, walking and running reshaped my leg muscles, strengthening and lengthening them.

Single-leg extension

RPM AND SPIN

Reps per minute (RPM) and spin are high-intensity cycling classes that are ideal for getting a woman's body into shape. They are especially good for people with injuries or back problems as they are very low-impact; being on a stationary bike, your core bears the majority of the weight. This form of exercise is ideal if you want to lose a large amount of weight, as you can increase your heart rate while your body is supported. Provided you maintain good posture on the bike, RPM and spin offer great cardio workouts with fewer injuries.

BE CONSISTENT

While it is important to factor in some rest time to avoid burnout, if you want to get the best body you've ever had, you have to train every day. That doesn't mean flogging yourself with high-intensity training each day, but it does mean moving regularly. If we allow ourselves to rest too much, it's easy to fall out of the habit of exercising. Very quickly, one day can turn into two, then into three, then, before you know it, a whole week has passed by and you've made no progress. Get your exercise groove on and focus on how good you feel when you move a bit every day.

Make a commitment to move every day

Water, water & more water

It is not an understatement to say that water is essential to life. We all know that. But it becomes even more important when we're training regularly.

Water flushes out and cleanses the body, removes fatty deposits, assists with cell growth and helps hydrate the skin. But how much should we drink? There is no exact science, as it depends on a number of variables: body size and composition, the weather, how much excerise we've done that day, and so on. However, a good rule of thumb is this: ⟶

Try it for yourself and see how you feel afterwards. Take particular note of your skin and I bet you will be hooked on hydration.

Of course, it is possible to drink too much water. Make sure that you don't consume more than 1 litre (4 cups) of water per hour, even if you're feeling thirsty. If you're finding that you want more, keep a water bottle on your desk or in your bag and sip it regularly throughout the day. Drinking too much water in one sitting can cause the level of salt in the blood to drop too low, leading to a condition called water intoxication.

WAKE UP

AT BREAKFAST

AT MORNING TEA

AT LUNCH

AFTER EXERCISE

AT DINNER

BEFORE BED

DURING THE DAY
sip water throughout the day, such as at your desk

Wellness

To me, overall wellness means maintaining a stable mind, mood, levels of energy and mobility. I achieve this through a personal regime of yoga, stretching and massage. It helps me to remain injury-free and well-aligned. Seeking this kind of holistic wellness is particularly important as we age. Regardless of whether you are young or more mature, remaining supple and aligned will better enable you to carry out your daily activities.

THE PITFALLS OF NOT STRETCHING INCLUDE:

- ✗ Pain in the muscles and joints
- ✗ Referred pain to smaller muscles from tight larger muscles
- ✗ Tight ligaments, leading to tearing
- ✗ Tired body
- ✗ Bad moods, anxiety
- ✗ Digestive and bowel problems, indigestion
- ✗ Body non-responsive to exercise.

My wellness activities include:

STRETCHING: DAILY (AFTER EVERY WORKOUT)

YOGA: WEEKLY OR FORTNIGHTLY
Yoga and pilates work by lengthening those muscles you have been reshaping.

MASSAGE: MONTHLY OR QUARTERLY
Massage is important for overall alignment. A full-body sports massage or lymphatic drainage massage (see page 58) will help flush the lactic acid and toxins from your body.

Find your strength

Alignment

Alignment is our body's biomechanical positioning. Being aligned means having proper posture, with all the muscles and bones moving correctly together. The dysfunction of alignment causes injury. An example of this is during pregnancy when a woman's pelvis moves to accommodate a growing baby. This then causes muscles and bones to expand and move, creating alignment issues within the body. Overcompensating for these weakened or misaligned muscles can cause longer-term problems.

> **Posture serves more purposes than just making you look taller. It engages all the major muscles in the body and keeps internal organs functioning properly.**

Good alignment is sexy. When our posture is good, we exude a magnetic energy and confidence. I saw a girl on Instagram who was in Vasisthasana, or side-plank pose. I found her instantly attractive because her alignment was spot on: her core was straight and strong, and she made it look effortless, like she was floating.

My posture got quite out of whack from carrying my babies. Although I was strong, this particular pose—where I would thrust my pelvis out in front with my legs bowed behind—resulted in the hyperflexion of my knees. I also injured my knee when I was training more seriously for triathlons. I recovered from these two connected and potentially serious problems by doing lots of yoga and by attending a number of sessions with a highly qualified therapist. My posture is now the best it has been in my life.

Old posture

New posture

Good alignment is sexy

Massage

There seems to be a lot of stigma attached to massage being a luxury item. Yet, if you consider all the benefits of a proper therapeutic massage, it is some of the best money you can spend on yourself. Massage can prevent injury, lessening the cost of medication and treatments such as physiotherapy or chiropractic therapies. It also helps reduce stress and avoid the build-up of tension and toxic waste in the body. Prevention really is better than cure. I try to book a massage at least once every three months, but monthly visits are ideal.

LYMPHATIC DRAINAGE MASSAGE

Feeling sluggish? Tired? Can't seem to shed that bit of fluid? A lymphatic massage will help. This one-hour gentle massage is relaxing yet highly therapeutic and produces astounding results in reshaping your body. It works by gently moving the fluid in the body towards the lymphatic glands, where it can be 'drained out' by your lymphatic system. It's performed by a qualified lymphatic massage therapist, and is particularly beneficial when the lymph nodes are blocked and the body is not capable of removing toxins on its own.

Not only does this massage improve the lymphatic system, but it also improves whole-body function, with proven benefits to the circulatory, respiratory and endocrine systems. It reduces the possibility of catching a cold or suffering a virus, and helps you lose unwanted weight and burn calories more effectively.

Finding a genuine lymphatic masseuse is a struggle, as many regular masseuses aren't properly trained in lymphatic drainage and use absurd techniques that have no purpose. Be sure to ask if the masseuse uses the Brazilian technique, as it is far superior to any other for flushing out toxins. (Hence why those Brazilian beauties have such amazing bodies; I knew there had to be a secret.)

My experience of lymphatic drainage

I personally aim to get a massage every three months to prevent ill-health; it's certainly cheaper to treat the cause than the symptoms. I have now added lymphatic drainage to my routine, and tend to use it before photo shoots and events, especially if I am feeling low and tired from work. Not only is this massage relaxing, but the fluid release is remarkable.

Find your strength

Pros & cons of lymphatic drainage

PROS

Increases energy.

+

Gives a feeling of lightness.

+

Helps you lean out.

+

Weight loss is visibly noticeable and muscles are more pronounced.

+

Improves body function (including bowel and urinary function).

CONS

Can give you bad breath and leave an odd taste in the mouth.

+

Can cause sweating or body odour the day after.

+

Can cause dehydration.

+

Can cause blotchy patches on the skin where the most intense flush has occurred.

+

May increase urgency for the toilet for up to 24 hours afterwards.

Note ☆ As lymphatic drainage causes the movement of fluids throughout the body, it is not recommended for anyone undergoing treatment for heart or kidney problems, or anyone having cancer treatment. Always consult your doctor before booking any kind of massage, including lymphatic drainage.

Yoga

Yoga is an Ayuverdic practice for developing the mind, body and spirit. In addition to strengthening our physical bodies, yoga teaches us self-awareness, wellbeing and how to recognise our potential. As we become more flexible, so too does our thinking, which, in turn, improves our relationship with ourselves and others. The development between softness and inner strength leads to a deeper understanding of ourselves and the universe, allowing us to think clearly and infuse our bodies with energy.

Yoga is the perfect complement to weight training and cardio. It sculpts the body and lengthens the muscles, making you look lean.

Yoga also helps to flush out lactic acid and toxins pooling in your muscles, so making it a part of your fitness routine is a no-brainer. I try to fit in one yoga or pilates session a week, and I love slowing down the pace for a moment and feeling the benefits of this practice, both for my body and soul.

The science of the body

The science of optimal body function has been studied for thousands of years, yet there still isn't one magic solution that solves all our body problems. Instead, the science behind fitness and good health is always evolving, and we are constantly seeking new ideas for weight loss, better nutrition and training principles. Often, we follow trends for certain diets or exercises in our pursuit of perfection, only to find that there is no evidence-based research to support them.

The one positive thing about trends is that they make people more aware of their options for health and fitness. There is so much information on the internet, in books, on forums and websites,

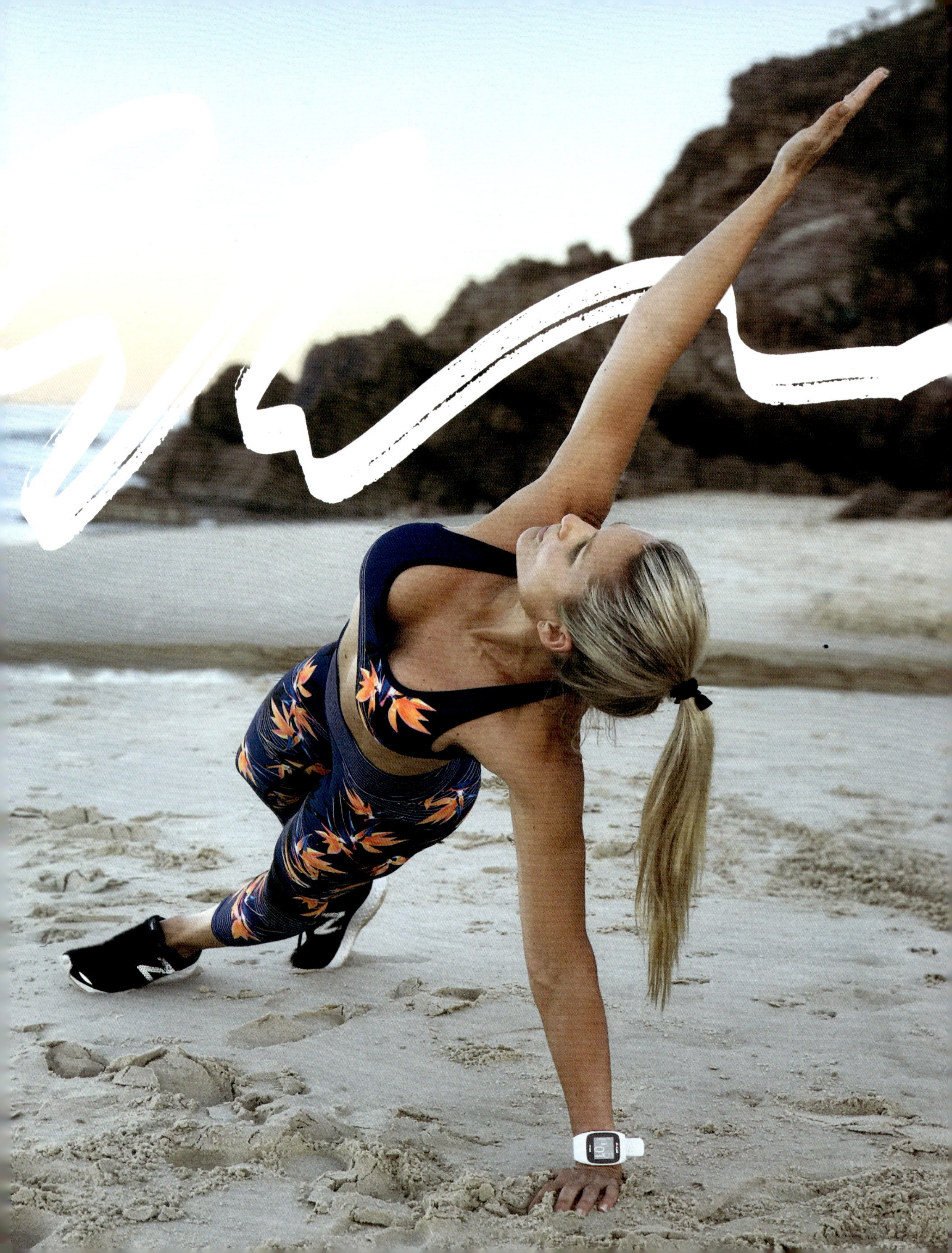

and even on social media that can help us on our path to better health, and many of these resources come from reputable and experienced individuals.

But with so much information out there, how do we know what advice to follow? No matter how many new diet trends or fitness fads there are, the science keeps pointing towards something very simple: a healthy balance of fresh, clean food and regular exercise.

There is no silver bullet and no short cut; no quick fix and no charcoal-infused, camel-milk, inca berry-topped latte that will do the job. Whether you consult a doctor, an elite athlete or a nutritionist, their advice is always pretty straightforward: eat well, move more, stress less.

This is what many refer to as the 'science of the body': the basic equation for keeping our bodies happy and our health on track. The general rule is that the calories we consume must be equal to the calories we expend. Any imbalance in calorie intake—either too few or too many—will make us put on or lose weight. Maintaining a calorie imbalance over many years can have serious detrimental effects on our health.

COUNTING CALORIES

Though it is tempting when trying to lose weight, counting calories can become obsessive. Some people keep food diaries, while others use apps to count their overall calorie intake as well as macronutrients, such as protein, carbohydrates, fat, sugar and salt. There is an argument for counting calories when you first begin, to help you learn the caloric values of the things you eat regularly. However, it is easy to develop a reliance on these technologies and stop 'listening' to your body. As soon as you have a grasp on the calories in most of the things that you eat, try to shift your focus away from counting every last crumb—it's not healthy or sustainable.

Eat well, move more, stress less

Find your strength 63

Relaxation

After a long day at work or at home with the kids, all we want to do is relax and unwind. Some of us want to escape with a glass of wine or indulge in our favourite treats. However, stocking up on alcohol and sugar is counterproductive when it comes to reducing stress. In fact, these two culprits (alongside caffeine) only make us feel more on edge.

Unwinding is about relaxing and regaining our balance and equilibrium, and there are good and bad ways to do it.

> First, we have to give ourselves permission to relax, which a lot of women find difficult.

Between children, work and household chores, some women feel selfish about taking time out, but it is essential to keep our bodies functioning optimally. It's better for our children, too; they would rather have a calm, relaxed mum than a burned-out, stressed one.

STRESS RELIEF

Stress is one of the biggest health concerns of the modern age. It has been linked to high blood pressure, heart disease, mental health disorders, seizures and obesity. Therefore, proactively decreasing stress should be a part of everyone's health and wellness routine.

Two of the best stress relievers are movement and breathing. They're such basic functions, so it's surprising how easily they can get out of rhythm, causing anxiety, depression, irritability and overbreathing. The act of 'resetting' our breath and motion through meditation, yoga, swimming or walking allows us to reconnect with the present. It is only once we have de-stressed that we are capable of clear and logical thought, and feel more like ourselves again.

Free yourself FROM NEGATIVE THOUGHTS

How to de-stress more effectively

1 CREATE PEACEFUL SPACES AT HOME. Use headphones to zone out external noise, lower the lighting and switch off technology.

2 LEAVE WORK AT THE OFFICE. Switch off your work phone and log out of your work email so you aren't tempted to check them for messages. Impose a cut-off time in the evening after which you agree with your family not to talk about work.

3 PAY ATTENTION TO YOUR BREATH. Find even just five minutes in a day when you can close your eyes, sit very still and focus entirely on your breath and the rise and fall of your stomach. Sometimes it helps to place a hand on your stomach so you can check your technique. (Yes, there is a technique to breathing.) Breathe in through your nose for a count of four, then slowly out through your mouth for a count of four. Finding this time can be difficult for mums, but tell your children that mum needs a few minutes to do something important. The more often you tell them, the more they will get used to leaving you alone while you do it. (This teaches them some independence, too.)

4 OBSERVE YOUR SURROUNDINGS. Switch off your devices and go for a walk in the evening, pausing to look at the lit-up homes, the tree-lined streets and the views. Appreciate the fresh air and the sensory experiences: hearing leaves rustling, feeling the cool air on your skin, the simple act of walking.

5 SLOW DOWN. The frantic must-get-it-all-done-now attitude is particularly hard for women to shirk. We are the queens of multitasking: helping the kids with their homework while on a call, while cooking dinner, while ironing school uniforms. And we're making ourselves crazy. These tasks aren't going anywhere, and you will do each one much better if you take them one at a time, so allow yourself a guilt-free breather when you get in the door before you launch into doing things. Just don't get trapped in front of the TV for two hours.

Ways to unwind

I personally choose to unwind with yoga, walking with the kids on the beach, or even meditating. In our house, the TV is rarely on. Instead, we tend to sit outside on our hanging chairs and discuss the day. I am truly blessed that my children see the benefits of a slow and peaceful life. That's not to say that they don't love technology (I sometimes switch off the wi-fi to make sure we have time to talk), but they always benefit from this downtime; they sleep soundly and have less anxious minds and bodies.

Find your strength

4

Find your confidence

CHANGE YOUR RELATIONSHIP WITH FOOD AND YOUR BODY

What we think and how we view the world directly impact our actions. If we are scared, we hold back; if we are confident, we move forwards. In order to achieve our goals, action and thought need to come together in perfect harmony. We need to positively visualise what we are aiming for and take active steps towards achieving it. Sometimes this will involve an attitude change away from negative patterns of self-talk and behaviour and towards more compassionate, targeted steps.

Looking after our bodies is not a luxury; it is a necessity, and we have to start viewing it that way. We must challenge the negative feelings that we have around eating and exercise, and repurpose them into something more helpful. Focusing first on strengthening the mind is a necessary step in order to change the body.

Become an early riser

As we age, we tend to need less sleep as we are using less energy throughout the day. But, when you are a busy working mum of two or three children, every wink of sleep counts. However, pause and think about how much time you spend rushing around, getting ready, grabbing a coffee and bustling the kids out the door. Is it really worth that extra half an hour in bed? Probably not.

Consider the lack of personal fulfilment you have during your waking hours. Having more sleep and less time during the day means having to cram a lot in, which leaves you feeling overwhelmed and unsatisfied with your life. Contrary to popular belief, a little less sleep and a little more quality time is actually a good way to combat fatigue. Getting up a bit earlier is a simple, practical strategy to reduce stress and discover a more peaceful, meaningful life. Sure, the first ten minutes will feel horrible but, once you are up and about, that feeling quickly wears off.

Another perk of becoming an early riser is that barely anyone is awake, so you can enjoy a few blissful minutes to yourself, whether to flow through a simple yoga routine, sit quietly on the couch,

Rise early → Combat fatigue + Reduce stress

quickly pack the school lunches or sip a hot (yes, hot!) cup of coffee. Many people have found this simple trick to be their greatest asset for living well.

Once you commit to rising a bit earlier, consider forming a morning routine. By that I don't mean kneeling before a ring of candles and praying to the sun god (unless that's your thing), I mean developing a set of behaviours or tasks for first thing in the morning that you repeat every day. Your routine might simply be to get up, stretch, shower and sit down to drink a coffee for ten minutes. Or, it might be more elaborate.

The point is to create a short, efficient routine that involves completing the same tasks each day to make your morning easier and more enjoyable.

Of course, women who are breastfeeding will benefit from more sleep and slightly increased calories to cope with the demand, so use your common sense and try to create a balance between having more time and giving your body the rest that it needs to fuel both you and your baby.

Creating a beautiful morning ritual will enhance the quality of your life and ensure you are making the most of each day.

Embrace your age

There's no denying that our society is obsessed with staying young as long as we can. We all have a picture in our heads of how we'd love to look. As we age, this picture seems to fade. As people reach their forties and fifties, feeling and looking young becomes a priority, and we begin to make alterations to our lives in the pursuit of youth. This may be especially true for ageing women who have had children. We start to resent our age and dwell on the past, when everything was better, healthier, brighter. But ageing is inevitable, and instead of wishing our autumn and winter years away, wouldn't it be easier and less stressful to embrace them and do the best we can with the body we've got?

What we often fail to acknowledge is that the loss of one body makes way for a new one. We might not be able to get our ideal bodies back, but we can celebrate our new bodies for what they look like and what they are capable of now.

The best way to celebrate our new body is to 'throw out' the image of the old one.

One of my techniques is to grab a clump of hair, visualise the old image and pull that image from your brain (give your hair a good tug; don't pull it right out). The sensation feels like you have removed something from your head. Now, throw it away. By creating space in your mind for something new, you can begin to embrace your current, powerful and just-as-worthy body.

Now, instead of rueing your wrinkles and cursing your grey hairs, look at what is within your power to change. Loss of muscle tone and changes to our skin and hair are unavoidable parts of ageing, but there are some things that are within our control, such as keeping fit and strong, and making the most of our looks. Aim to keep active and mobile, and treat yourself to new clothes and nice hair styles; getting older needn't spell disaster.

Even small changes can make a world of difference to how we look and feel. We can't turn back the clock, but we can learn to make the most of where we are today and be grateful for it.

THE PAY-OFF OF GOOD HEALTH

Can you put a price on your health? No? Well, you do if you prefer to pay for medications rather than focusing on eating better and moving more to improve your general health. This is the ultimate

Small changes make a world of difference

choice for many: either pay out for a fast fix or do the work. The less we value our health, the more money we end up having to spend on drugs to improve it. In the process, we diminish our quality of life. We risk our jobs, our goals and our families all because we are too lazy to make sensible choices about our diet and exercise. We can either choose foods that nourish us and enhance our health, and move our bodies daily to keep them functional, or we can eat cheap, 'fast' food, move less and spend more on medications. In the long run, it's easier—and cheaper—to just be healthy.

Of course, many people suffer health problems that are outside of their control. If you must take medication for a health condition, work with your doctor to supplement your treatment by practising good general health. By that I mean, make sure all the basics are covered: eat good-quality, nourishing food, drink plenty of water and move regularly. It might help with your health condition or it might not, but it will certainly improve your general health, making your body better able to cope with chronic health problems. (For more about healthy eating, see pages 144–203.)

SLOW AGEING BY REDUCING STRESS

Stress is a fact of life for most people, but the truth is, it is making us ill. The longer we endure stress, the more it impacts our health. Unfortunately, not all stress can be avoided, so it isn't as simple as saying that we should 'stop' being stressed. But what we can control is how we manage and reduce our stress.

Being in a stressed or anxious state can make us age prematurely. When we feel stressed or threatened, we trigger our bodies to release the hormones cortisol and adrenaline, which can disrupt normal bodily functions and send confused messages to the brain. Instead of flowing freely, blood is pumped to the digestive system; muscle breakdown takes place, and the body stops burning fat efficiently. Combined, all of these effects can cause premature ageing, not just of our skin and hair, but of our internal organs, too.

Stop weighing yourself

The happiest, most balanced women usually have this in common: they do not weigh themselves. They do not allow a number on a scale to dictate how their day will go, their self-worth or how they feel.

Growing up, we never had a pair of scales in our bathroom at home, but my aunties and grandparents did. Their scales fascinated me. When I was racing, my life was ruled by the number on the scales and counting calories—to my detriment. Every day depended on what number rolled over the pointer: what a horrible way to start a day. It broke my confidence and made me question my abilities.

It took me a while to realise it, but I came to see that the number on the scales doesn't matter. It never has and it never will. I weigh around 62 kg now, but that's just a guess as I tend not to weigh myself anymore. Depending on the time of the month and how my digestive system is performing, my weight can vary between 58 kg and 62 kg.

My body composition is excellent. I feel healthy and energised, and my mobility is in tiptop shape. I feel happier than I ever have, largely because I have not weighed myself in years and I never will again.

RID THE WORD 'DIET' FROM YOUR VOCABULARY

The one word that is killing our love of food is 'diet'. Dieting means reducing and restricting foods. However, if we are choosing to eat good-quality, wholesome foods, then we don't need to restrict what we eat. Freeing ourselves from this word means that we can begin to rebuild our relationship with food, and eat and move in ways that are beneficial—not detrimental—to our bodies.

I love good, wholesome food. I love its flavour, its smells and its textures, and loving the right foods in this way has given me my life back. It's given me back all the hours I spent counting every single calorie. I now focus on eating a balanced combination of vegetables, fruits, lean proteins, good-quality carbohydrates and plenty of water. It's really quite simple.

The happiest women don't weigh themselves

Find your confidence 75

Change the way you think about food

I used to use food to improve my mood and to help me get moving in the morning. I used food as a reward, as a way to make me happy or to impress others. I used to fall victim to the latest food crazes and trends. Essentially, I lost sight of the correct way to think about food.

You've only got to look on social media to see the current obsession with sugar-loaded, highly addictive food. There are hashtags for #foodporn and #cheatmeal, and Instagram is plastered with photos of 'freakshakes' and oozy burgers. The subliminal message is that it's okay to eat these things, but it's not.

In between the latest food crazes, advertising, cooking shows and social media, working out where (the right) food fits into our lives is difficult. We stop seeing food as fuel and start seeing it as a commodity, or another 'trend' that we must follow. Temptation is all around us, and the line between what is good for our bodies and what we want is constantly blurred. But we must work hard to resist it and, more importantly, we have to teach our children to do the same. It's time to reassess our relationship with food.

To change the way we think about food, we must first examine the most common mistakes we make. For example, one common mistake is overstating our need for food:

- ✘ 'I'm exhausted. I need that big bowl of cheesy pasta.'
- ✘ 'I can't help it, I'm addicted to chocolate.'
- ✘ 'But wine is the only thing that helps me to relax.'
- ✘ 'I don't eat much sugar, so it's okay to have more bread.'
- ✘ 'I have to have that piece of cake or I'll die!'

We grant ourselves permission to eat or drink the things we shouldn't, and we do it so often that we start to believe these statements are true. In reality, it is not the chocolate or chips or sugar we're craving, but energy and carbohydrates. In order to stop overeating the wrong foods, we have to figure out why we're craving them and then look at healthier alternatives. For example, many people enjoy a glass of wine while cooking dinner, saying it helps them to relax. I bet that if you replaced that glass of wine with some deep-breathing exercises and fresh mineral water, you would feel just as relaxed.

Our minds are amazing. They are programmed to support routines and habits, but it only takes a few weeks for our minds to adapt to change, so it's important to persevere with the positive changes you want to make. Being aware of your eating patterns and the things you say to yourself is the first step. The second is to challenge them with more helpful self-talk, such as 'I am not really going to die if I don't have that piece of cake. It's full of sugar and white flour and other empty calories that will do nothing for my body but make it gain weight.' The third step is to put these thoughts into action. Yes, it will be difficult at first, but you will soon get the hang of it, and the rewards will speak for themselves.

CONQUERING CRAVINGS

We all have cravings and sometimes they are difficult to manage, as they're almost always for high-fat, high-sugar foods that we know we shouldn't eat. I get these cravings, too, and, when they hit, I take the following steps:

A word on chewing: there's more to it than you think. Yes, you need to chew your food in order to swallow it, but the rate at which you chew has remarkable effects, too. The action of chewing slowly releases endorphins—the happy hormones—making us feel satisfied. It also helps to reduce the amount you eat overall.

Tips to curb cravings

1

Find a healthy alternative

2

If I can't find a healthy alternative, I'll try to at least find a healthier version of the same food.

3

If neither of the first two steps is possible, I will have a bite—just one bite—of whatever I'm craving. I chew it slowly, concentrating on its flavour, and this usually satisfies me.

Chewing slowly releases happy hormones

CARBS ARE NOT EVIL

Many diets point to carbs as the enemy, so much so that many of us try to avoid them at all costs. But, in the process, we are missing out on valuable nutrients and starches that are essential to our brain and body function. That said, not all carbs were created equal, and knowing the 'rules' behind eating them is key.

Tips for eating good carbs

- ★ Aim for carbohydrates made with whole grains. Breads, crackers and wraps that are high in grains and seeds will keep you feeling full for longer. Whole grains are also good roughage, which assists with digestion.

- ★ Always measure servings of carbohydrates to make sure you are not exceeding a normal portion. For cereal, muesli, rice and pasta, that's usually ½–1 cup per meal.

- ★ Always eat carbohydrates with protein. For example, have your muesli with yoghurt, your rice with chicken, or your crackers with tinned tuna.

- ★ Limit your carbohydrates from fruit. Fruit is high in carbohydrates, so don't eat more than two to three pieces a day and make sure you have some protein with it, such as nuts, yoghurt or cheese.

PROTEIN

Protein has many benefits: it stabilises blood sugar, keeps cravings away, keeps you feeling full and helps you build muscle. It's an essential macronutrient, especially if you are trying to lose weight. The main sources of protein include meat, poultry, fish, seafood and dairy, as well as good-quality, free-range eggs.

Adding a high-quality supplementary protein powder to your diet is a great way to make sure you're getting enough protein throughout the day. It's especially beneficial when consumed immediately after a workout, as it helps to repair and strengthen muscles, and keeps your metabolism high. I use a lean whey chocolate protein. It helps with my chocolate cravings and is perfect for that mid-afternoon dip in energy.

TOO MUCH MEAT

As a population, we eat too much meat, but it's red meat that has the biggest impact on our bodies. Red meats are more difficult to digest, and some people's stomach acid isn't strong enough to properly break them down. While red meat does contain a lot of iron, it is not the only food source for this important mineral. Leafy green vegetables, blueberries, sultanas, dried apricots, legumes, nuts and seeds are all high in iron, and are particularly important for those suffering from iron deficiency.

If you eat red meat regularly, you might not even notice how it makes you feel. Next time you eat it, pay close attention to your body afterwards. Notice any bloating and digestive discomfort and have a think about whether you would benefit from reducing your consumption of red meat or cutting it out entirely.

Healthy sources of protein include:

Handful of cooked, shredded chicken or turkey

Small handful of plain, unsalted nuts or seeds

Unsweetened, full-fat yoghurt

Nut or cow's milk

Tofu or tempeh

Eggs

Pulses and beans, such as black beans, navy beans and chickpeas

TOO MUCH SUGAR

Ah, the white stuff. For so long, doctors and nutritionists—even governments—failed to see that sugar was wreaking havoc on our health, contributing to various diseases including heart disease and stroke, Type-2 diabetes and an obesity pandemic. Now, everywhere you turn, health professionals implore you to drastically reduce or, better still, eradicate sugar completely from your diet.

Yet, we can't seem to leave it alone. We feel we need it. Why? Because sugar is addictive, and it produces the same reward- and pleasure-effect as drugs and alcohol. If you really want to lose weight and regain your health, you have to leave it behind—in all its forms. Replacing it with sweet alternatives such as dates, bananas and smoothies will help, but many of these can also cause problems. The best approach is to reduce your sugar intake to a bare minimum and, when you do crave it, try to find healthy replacements and consume them in very small amounts.

Healthy sugar swaps

HONEY: A natural alternative to white, refined sugar. Honey has a host of other benefits, too, including hayfever relief and antibacterial properties, especially Manuka honey.

RICE MALT SYRUP: A credible alternative to maple syrup (which is very high in sugar), rice malt syrup, or RMS, is made from cultured brown rice that is cooked until it breaks down into a syrup.

NATURAL, PLANT-BASED SWEETENERS, SUCH AS STEVIA OR NATVIA: Sugar substitutes made from the leaf of the stevia plant.

Find your confidence

Portion sizes and overeating

Unfortunately, many of us were brought up to consume excessive amounts of food. As children, we were not allowed to leave the table until we'd finished every last piece of food on our plate (often normal-sized dinner plates with far too much food). Over time, we came to see this as the norm, and many people have carried this over into adulthood. But the truth is that we simply don't need to consume vast amounts of food. It might feel good to do so, but it actually has serious ramifications.

Do you ever feel bloated? Sick or lethargic after eating? Do you have mood swings? It could be due to overeating. When we overeat, our stomachs go into overdrive trying to process the food, our heart rate increases and our metabolism slows.

Overeating is a common problem in the developed world. Food keeps getting larger (as well as sweeter, saltier and fattier) to entice you to buy it. This tricks our primitive brains, which are programmed to avoid starvation at all costs, into wanting to eat as much as possible. Luckily, you can override your primal urges by working out the correct portion size for yourself. Our stomachs are approximately the size of both our fists placed side by side. This is what your own, individual portion size should look like. This is true from birth all the way into adulthood. Therefore, your baby or child only needs as much food as is equal to their two clenched fists.

Now that you have your portion size, you can work out how to split your food up throughout the day. I eat six small meals of highly nutritious, delicious fresh food every day, as I find that eating frequent small portions keeps my blood sugar and metabolism stable, and keeps me feeling energised.

The repercussions of overeating

The consequences of overeating are widespread and profound, causing physiological reactions within the body. It can lead to:

Bloating and acid-induced ulcers
+
Heartburn
+
Stomach pain and excess stomach acid
+
Fatigue
+
Mood swings
+
Food dependency and addiction
+
Weight gain
+
Sugar cravings
+
Exacerbation of pre-existing health conditions, such as irritable bowel syndrome

1 container = x3

Tips to avoid overeating

USE A SMALL PLATE. This tricks your brain into thinking there is more food.

BEWARE OF TAKEAWAY CONTAINERS. If you place food from the container into a small bowl, you'll often find it contains almost three servings, not one.

USE SMALL SNACK CONTAINERS. Little containers for kids' lunchboxes are perfect—even for fully grown men.

TAKE CARE OF THE 1 PER CENTS. Focus on cutting out the seemingly insignificant things, such as the extra scrape of butter on your toast, that half a biscuit, the sugar in your tea or coffee, and the generous glugs of olive oil.

QUALITY OVER QUANTITY

Everything you eat should provide your body with nutrients and energy. It's easy for exhausted new mums to reach for convenient, high-sugar, high-carb foods, but while these empty calories might fill you up or satisfy a craving, the effects are short-lived and it's not long before you go in search of another snack. By reconnecting with your love of good-quality food, you can address these bad habits and better nourish yourself and your child.

Find your confidence 83

Tips for good eating habits

RENAME FOOD. Stop thinking of foods as either 'good' or 'bad', and assign them different names, such as 'nourishing' and 'treat', etc.

MINIMISE INDULGENCE. Don't make every meal an excuse to eat something special. Try to stick to plain foods during the week, with a treat or special-occasion meal once a week.

NEVER HAVE TWO TREAT DAYS IN A ROW. It's fine to have a treat day occasionally, but make sure you follow it up with a healthy day of eating the next day.

STOP HIDING FOOD. We all do it, but it's a habit that needs to be broken. Those little bits of biscuit and sips of cola all add up. Move your food—especially the treats—into plain sight, so that you can hold yourself more accountable.

DON'T EAT IN THE CAR OR IN FRONT OF THE TV. We tend to zone out when we're driving or watching TV and, before we know it, half a block of chocolate is gone. Be present in your food choices and eat at the table away from distractions.

DON'T SHOP WHEN HUNGRY. If you go to the supermarket when you're hungry or have skipped a meal, you will almost certainly end up buying things you don't need, as well as coming out of the shop with snacks for the ride home.

DON'T GORGE BEFORE DINNER. Grazing on cheese and biscuits or the dinner ingredients will mean that you won't fill up on the nutritious meal. Distract yourself with the kids or chores until dinner is ready.

STOP EATING THE KIDS' LEFTOVERS. If you are watching your portion sizes, don't undo all the hard work by adding another half a plateful from the kids' leftovers.

Five tips for eating out

Eating dinner out is an enjoyable activity for most people, but for those wanting to lose weight, it can be a source of stress. Here are some tips for eating out without putting your progress in jeopardy.

1. **ALWAYS MAKE THE FIRST BITE RAW FOOD, THEN FOLLOW IT UP WITH PROTEIN.** Carbohydrates only fuel your appetite.

2. **EAT SLOWLY, LIKE A RESTAURANT CRITIC.** Try to savour the taste of your food.

3. **DON'T FILL UP ON BREAD.** If you do eat bread before a meal, stick to wholegrain bread and eat less of it. Avoid butter or too many dips in the olive oil.

4. **SIP WATER BETWEEN COURSES.** This will help fill you up and counter the effects of alcohol.

5. **STOP WHEN YOU'RE FULL.** Sometimes it's hard to leave food when you've paid for an expensive dinner out, but don't force-feed yourself. It's okay to leave some on the plate.

Find your confidence 85

Change your relationship with junk food

Once you become a mum, food and cooking become a central part of life, if they were not already. A lot of time is spent cooking, shopping and meal-planning, as well as talking about food with hungry children. And, as a new mother, you are constantly looking for quick sources of energy so, when you do get a chance to eat, it's all too easy to reach for junk food.

One of the main complaints I hear from clients wanting to lose weight is that they can't stop thinking about eating—and weight-loss programs don't help. In fact, all they do is make you focus on food even more: how many calories you've consumed, what your macros are, how many treats you've had, and so on. It quickly becomes obsessive and then you wonder why you've failed. So you give up, feel guilty, throw it in the 'too hard' basket and return to your KitKat.

In order to shed the mum-bod and rediscover a healthier way of eating and living, you need to restore your love of real food. Remember? The stuff you used to eat before a screaming baby robbed you of all your energy. Re-educating yourself on what foods to eat is much easier when you focus on the effects they have on your body. Do you want to eat something that makes you feel sluggish and bloated? Or something that makes you feel energised and clear?

TOXIC FOODS

As well as containing zero useful calories or nutrients, junk food is highly toxic, filled with artificial flavours, E numbers, colours and preservatives—chemicals that our bodies don't know how to process and that can cause illness and allergic reactions. They are also highly addictive, making us crave them even more. In my experience, it takes about ten days to 'reset' our palates after eating something like this, so it is better avoided altogether. The toxins in unhealthy foods create a variety of adverse bodily effects. They often begin with basic discomforts, such as stomach aches, bloating, reflux, bad breath, fatigue and indigestion. Left too long in the body, toxins can lead to blocked arteries, high cholesterol and stomach ulcers. In the long run, this can add up to heart disease, strokes and a wide range of gastrointestinal issues as your body overcompensates to remove the toxins.

HOW I BROKE UP WITH JUNK FOOD

I was the same as many of you: eating the crusts off my children's sandwiches for 'breakfast', sipping the last of the juice so it didn't sit in the fridge for weeks, and having the last few squares of chocolate to avoid any arguments.

Do any of these excuses sound familiar to you?

I am tired. This will give me energy.
+
One bite doesn't count.
+
The kids' snack food is healthy, so I can eat that.
+
I've already eaten a handful of chips, so a few more won't hurt.
+
I can't waste this food.
+
I don't have time to eat properly.
+
When driving from place to place, I need something to keep me going.
+
They only sell junk at the service station, so what choice do I have?

I have used all of these and more. However, it is possible to change this self-talk and stop making excuses. To do this, I had to stop looking at food as just another chore and start consciously appreciating it again. Here's how I did it:

✯ I took notice of every single thing I put into my mouth. If you wanted to, you could even write it down and take a look at the end of the day—but if you do this, be real with yourself and record everything, and I mean everything.

✯ I visualised every mouthful giving me total body nourishment.

✯ I drank a glass of water before every meal.

✯ I created a simple, achievable meal plan of easy but healthy dinners that are quick and straightforward to cook.

✯ I ate almost exactly the same meals every week. It might sound boring, but it frees you from having to think about food too much and reduces temptation.

✯ I broke food down into its components. I still use this trick today to help keep me on track (see page 88).

Breaking food down into its individual ingredients helps you visualise what actually goes into it. For example, cheese is not just 'cheese'; it is fat, dairy and salt. What about chips? They're made of tiny slices of potato, salts, synthetic flavours and trans fats. Sounding good? Not to me. I would also try to think of how each food would make me feel. If I knew I would be struggling with constipation the next day, it made it easier to say no to the cheese.

Here are a couple to try for yourself:

Still want the junk?

I live entirely on oats, blueberries, almond milk, coffee, bananas, chicken, salmon, salad, broccoli, eggs, spinach, beetroot, sweet potatoes, pumpkin, quinoa and peanut butter. My body thrives on a balanced intake of these clean, healthy foods that provide me with vast amounts of energy.

Many people interpret 'eating a balanced diet' as having a little bit of everything they want (junk included). But what it really means is that you should eat a varied range of healthy food from different food groups, including proteins, carbohydrates, fats, fruits, vegetables and fibre.

And don't worry: it's okay to have moments of weakness. Just be sure to counter them by planning and preparing wholesome snacks to have on the run. Over time, this will create new habits and a new internal dialogue around food.

CHOCOLATE

COCOA BUTTER, COCOA SOLIDS, SUGAR, FLAVOURS, PALM OIL.

Does it leave a nasty residue in my mouth?
Yes.
Is it worth it?
No.

SOFT DRINK

SUGAR (A HELL OF A LOT), WATER, COLOUR, FLAVOURING, E NUMBERS, CARBONATED WATER, HIGH-FRUCTOSE CORN SYRUP.

Empty calories?
Yes.
In fact, soft drinks are one of the worst culprits for weight gain. Avoid them at all costs.

Feel good on the inside, look good on the outside

Women, and especially mothers, often find it hard to feel good about themselves. Between social media, hormone fluctuations, a lack of sleep and an ever-changing body shape, they are constantly fighting an uphill battle with their confidence and self-esteem. But in order to look good on the outside, we must first feel good from within.

Constant negative self-talk and comparing ourselves to others leaves us feeling convinced that we aren't motivated enough, attractive enough or worthy enough. However, a simple shift in attitude can lead to an increase in confidence, making us feel and look beautiful.

CLOTHES FOR CONFIDENCE

Confidence isn't something we're born with. We have to cultivate it with positive thinking, the people we choose to surround ourselves with and the choices we make. As new mothers, it isn't always easy to feel confident in yourself. After all, you're haggard and stressed, and there's very little time for bodily maintenance. One easy place to start is by dressing in clothes that flatter and celebrate your body shape, which can leave you feeling more confident in no time.

HERE ARE A FEW TIPS FOR DRESSING WITH CONFIDENCE:

- Wear the things you love.
- Accentuate your assets. You know what they say: if you've got it, flaunt it.
- Wear clothes that properly fit your waist.
- Focus on your posture.
- Don't ignore the details: nails, hair, eyebrows and make-up.
- Invest in beautiful lingerie.
- Get a haircut that flatters your face shape.
- Smile.

Eight tips for buying activewear

Over many years of doing photo shoots for activewear, I've developed an eye for shapes and lines. With all the exercise I've done, I've also learned what to look for in terms of utility. Here are my eight tips for finding the right activewear for your body type, even if you haven't caught the exercise bug yet.

1 When buying leggings, look for ones with as few seams as possible. These will make you look leaner and give your body a better silhouette. High-waisted leggings are great for giving support and accentuating feminine curves.

2 Look for high-quality fabrics. You are going to be sweating a lot, so buy activewear made of breathable, high-tech fabrics that don't pill or sag.

3 If you want to appear taller, wear full-length leggings, as these will make your body appear leaner, whereas three-quarter-length leggings and shorts make your body appear shorter and rounder.

4 Stick to block colours or full patterns, not panelled or patterned sections.

5 Pale colours are less forgiving and are best worn on the top half of the body.

6 The most flattering colours for activewear are black or bright colours and leopard prints.

7 The best crop tops are the ones that give you the most coverage across your décolletage. A scooped neck also creates the illusion of a longer torso.

8 Remove any inbuilt padding from activewear, as it moves while you're wearing it and tends to wash badly.

THE BENEFITS OF A BEAUTY ROUTINE

Before I discovered the healthy lifestyle I lead today, I was living off fast sugars, fatty snacks and toxic foods. My skin lost its elasticity and, from around the age of 30, I started getting wrinkles. The junk food I was eating directly affected my looks, so I cleaned up my act. Eating healthier food definitely improved my skin, bloating and my energy levels, and I began to feel motivated to adopt a beauty routine. This was a game-changer and really helped with my self-esteem.

My must-buy beauty products

- Good-quality face and body moisturiser, preferably an almond- or coconut oil-based one
- Serum
- Exfoliant and exfoliating mitt
- Loofah
- Rosehip oil
- Waterproof mascara

My beauty regime

DAILY

Thoroughly remove make-up.

+

Use a good-quality, paraben-free moisturiser. (I like almond oil-based moisturisers, which give an extra boost of nourishment.)

+

Use rosehip oil underneath the eyes.

+

Drink green tea.

+

Stay hydrated.

THREE TIMES A WEEK

Use a loofah to slough off dead skin cells.

+

Tidy eyebrows.

+

Trim and file nails.

WEEKLY

Exfoliate. I use an exfoliant that contains lactic acid, as it helps to remove toxins and maintain the skin's ideal pH.

+

Shave and moisturise using a moisturiser that contains vitamin E to maximise skin hydration and nourishment. I like to do this on a Thursday night so that I'm ready for the weekend.

+

Soak in a warm bath and give myself a facial. I like to do this on a Sunday night to prepare for the week ahead.

Find your confidence

Water flushes toxins and fatty deposits from the body

CELLULITE

Cellulite occurs when fatty deposits break through the connective tissue in our thighs and bum, giving the skin a dimpled appearance. Most women have it, and most women want to get rid of it. The answer? Diet. What we eat is up to 80 per cent responsible for cellulite production, and the only solution is to eat clean. Eating a well-balanced diet of lean proteins, lots of vegetables and leafy greens, and some quinoa and rice for carbohydrates, will help to improve cellulite.

After the age of 30, our bodies change dramatically. We process sugar differently, and those beloved 'treat' foods stick to our bodies like glue. The only way to enjoy overall health and avoid the repercussions of a bad diet is to eat clean, nutritious food.

My top six secret cellulite shredders

We've all got them—those lumps that seem to appear from nowhere, usually just in time for the summer. But don't despair. In addition to eating a healthy diet, there are some other things you can do to help.

1 SPEED WEIGHT CIRCUITS. These fast-paced sessions combine high repetitions with light weights to melt fat. Incorporate them into your fitness routine a couple of times a week.

2 WATER. Hydrating with water will flush toxins and fatty deposits from the body. It also helps with the dreaded bloat. When you're not drinking enough fluids, your body retains water to prevent it from dehydrating, so frequently drinking water throughout the day actually reduces bloat.

3 CARDIO. Complete a 30-minute cardio session every day before breakfast. Without fail. Either walk, run, cycle or do a mini functional-fitness circuit. Cardio exercise helps to target stubborn fat stores in the hips, thighs and lower back.

4 PROTEIN. Add a protein shake to your post-workout routine, and drop in another one mid-afternoon to help fight the blood-sugar dip. This will help you avoid high-sugar foods, which will only contribute to the cellulite.

5 YOGA. Enjoy a yoga or pilates class once a week. The strong, powerful movements increase blood flow around the body and help to flush out lactic-acid build-up. Stretching your muscles also helps them empty their fatty deposits into the bloodstream.

6 MASSAGE AND EPSOM SALT BATHS. These two easy and relaxing activities help flush toxins from the body. Book in a massage at least every three months, if not every month, and add a handful of Epsom salts to a hot bath to help with fluid retention. Massage, in particular, helps to direct fatty deposits towards the lymph nodes where they can be drained.

Find your confidence 93

CHOOSE love & compassion OVER JUDGMENT

PRAISE OTHERS

There is a reason why people say that beauty is only skin deep. A person might look great on the outside, but that doesn't necessarily translate to their character.

Complimenting others costs nothing, and it's a great way to show off your positive character. Have you ever read an article or online post and thought, 'that's really thought-provoking'? Well, why not tell the author?

There is plenty of love, praise and positivity to go around, and acknowledging the success of others only takes a second out of your day.

As women, we spend a lot of time putting each other down. Instead of expending energy on negativity and judgment, we should be channelling it into building one another up. The next time you spot a struggling mum, don't judge her unwashed hair or unmanicured fingernails. Instead, think about what a great job she's doing with her children or, better still, tell her. I guarantee you will make her day.

I try to avoid putting others down at all costs, but occasionally I feel jealousy and judgment creeping in. When I do, I remind myself of the following things:

- We are all on our own unique journeys. My job is to focus on mine.
- If I feel angry, to stop and appreciate the things that are right in front of me, whether that's a beautiful view or the car in front.
- If I feel sad, to stop and look at my children. Be proud of the beautiful souls I have created and how much love surrounds me.

No matter what situation you are in, always remember to look around. Look for all the positive things in your life, look for a smile, look for compassion. No one can make your life good or bad except you. It is your responsibility to choose love and compassion over judgment.

Find your confidence

5

Find your balance

MIND OVER MATTER

So, you've worked out your priorities and set your goals. You've committed to a training program and a wellness routine. You've even tried to overhaul your thinking around food. But what about your motivation? What about the number-one thing that holds people back? Fear.

Sometimes the things we fear can be acknowledged and dealt with. Other times, they're here to stay, so we have no choice but to brace ourselves and work through them. This is mind over matter: fearing something but doing it anyway.

In order to lead a happy life, we have to do one or the other, and making the effort to understand why you feel the way you do is an important step in learning to let go of fear.

You're starting a new phase of your life—a healthier one in which you plan to become the woman and mother you've always dreamed of being. So why can't you find the will to start? It's probably fear that is standing in your way. Fear of failing, fear of being judged, or fear that it just won't work. Sound familiar?

Learning to challenge unhelpful thinking and navigate the emotional roller-coaster of starting something new will help you on the road to success.

Confirmation bias

Confirmation bias is when we search for information that confirms our bias. For example, if we believe that we are overweight, we will interpret information, people's comments and our own self-talk as confirmation, and reject anything that doesn't fit with our beliefs. This can be detrimental to our mental health, as it does not always reflect reality.

Learning to recognise confirmation bias is the first step towards overcoming it, and it might not be as easy as you think. Many of our beliefs, especially negative ones about our bodies, are so deeply ingrained that they morph into 'facts', whether or not they are true.

Women are so critical of themselves and their bodies, and this can often lead to body dysmorphia, a mental-health condition where we obsess over what we perceive to be a flaw when, in actual fact, there is absolutely nothing wrong with us.

Instead of looking for reasons to confirm the worst parts of yourself, consider what people around you are saying. If someone says you look great in that dress, simply say thank you. Accept the compliment graciously, and don't question it or immediately respond with all the reasons why it is not true. Challenge those unhelpful thoughts, and weigh up how realistic your bias is.

Getting motivated

When it comes to living a healthier life, motivation is the biggest hurdle most people face. We have trouble starting, then make a small start that we maintain for a few days or weeks, but then, things get too hard. We can't commit to the schedule, we get bored or just decide it isn't for us. Very quickly, old, unhealthy habits return.

If you really want to change your life, it requires commitment and determination. There is no easy way around it; you have to do the work. Take the muscle-bound guy that you see at the gym every morning. He's definitely had times when he wanted to hit 'snooze' on his alarm. He's had times when he couldn't be bothered and the last place he felt like being was the gym. But he's still there six days a week. Why does he have so much motivation and you don't? The truth is, he doesn't. He's just made a pact with himself to be consistent until he reaches his goals.

Sometimes setting goals takes you outside your comfort zone. For instance, my journey was prompted by a mixture of strong emotions, and not all of them were positive. I felt frustrated that the clothes I wore before giving birth didn't fit anymore. I was sick of looking tired and feeling unwell all the time. I wanted to be myself again.

Accept compliments graciously

Find your balance 99

NO MORE EXCUSES

Many of us make excuses to ourselves every day to justify our behaviour. We didn't go to the gym because we were too tired. We ate that muffin because we didn't have time for breakfast.

In order to get motivated, we have to stop making excuses. We have to be honest with ourselves and take a long, hard look at how our current behaviour serves our goals. If you ate the muffin, own up to it, admit that it was detrimental to your weight-loss efforts and move on. It's only once we make ourselves accountable like this that we can motivate ourselves to change.

Many new mothers make excuses for not fitting exercise into their day: they're tired, busy and have to look after a baby. This might sound harsh, but there are plenty of women out there doing all of these things and managing to make time for fitness. It's a question of value. If you place as much value on your own health and fitness as you do on looking after your baby and catching up on sleep, then you will make it work.

Only once you have freed yourself from excuses will you be able to focus on your goals. Decide what they will be and get moving.

Fight your fears

Being scared is something I felt my entire life until four years ago when I started my own business. I got past my fear because my desire to help people was greater than my fear. Prior to that, I was always scared: scared of not being good enough, or that I would be judged. I was almost scared of my own shadow. But fear is like diving under a wave; if you don't, you'll be tossed under. If you do, you will come out the other side.

Remember that, typically, the thing you want is on the other side of fear. You must do the things you think you cannot do to get it.

> *Challenging your fears is the beginning of true freedom*

WHY DO WE EXPERIENCE FEAR?

There are many reasons why we experience fear, but at least a part of it is that we are physiologically programmed that way. As humans evolved, fear was the difference between being eaten by a lion or killing it. Because of our hunter-gatherer ancestors, fear is in our DNA. We are wired to sniff out danger and threats, and we react with either fight or flight—that is, to either stand and face our fear or run away.

This fight-or-flight response is essential to our survival. Without it, we wouldn't react to the dangers around us, which could lead to injury or death. Unfortunately, for some people, this fight-or-flight response goes into overdrive, causing anxiety. Generalised anxiety disorder is a condition where people feel worried and anxious most of the time, not just when they are in dangerous situations. People with this disorder often find it difficult to carry out even the most basic daily tasks, but even this level of fear can be challenged, if not eliminated.

Women, especially, experience fear. We worry about our safety, about being a failure, about ageing and dying, and about whether we are good mothers to our children. We fear not getting what we want out of life and losing what we have. Then we increase our fear even further by being fearful of fear itself.

However, we cannot define ourselves by our fears; it restricts our world and makes us question our sanity. Learning to face them is hard, but the more we do it the more we realise that the thing we fear is not as bad as we thought; that the sensation of fear quickly dissipates and becomes more manageable.

LEARN TO LET GO

Letting go of fear takes education, practice and patience. It's not going to happen overnight, but it will happen.

Watching our children is proof that it is possible to live without fear. My daughter has no fear at all. In fact, she is so fearless that she is even more determined than me sometimes. She actually taught herself how to do yoga poses. I remember holding her in a position and she just said, 'Let go'. I feared her falling, but I let go. She was absolutely fine. Of course, as you get older and you have learned a bit about the world, fear increases, but this doesn't mean that it should rule your life.

Letting go of fear is a huge obstacle for most people, but the perception of fear is nothing more than an illusion we have constructed. So what if we fall? We get back up. If we need to apologise, we do. If we are embarrassed, we shake it off. Nothing is ever quite as bad as we expect it to be.

> *Part of letting go of fear is being comfortable with giving up control.*

As adults, we feel we must control every situation, but this only feeds our anxiety when we cannot control everything. It's impossible to stop random bad things from happening, and the sooner we get comfortable with this idea, the better. We don't know how everything is going to turn out, but we must try our best anyway. I once read a quote from the young poet Erin Hanson that really resonated with me: '"What if I fall?" Oh but my darling, what if you fly?'

INTUITION AND SELF-DOUBT

Intuition, or your gut feeling, is like a personal light bulb that goes off in your head. We use our intuition when working out a problem and meeting new people, and it's an important tool to hone.

Looking back, I realise that I have had intuition about every major event in my life. Before I learned to trust this instinct, though, I made many mistakes and wrong choices. Once I tuned in to what my gut was telling me, things started to fall into place.

Intuition and self-doubt are so intertwined. You want to follow your gut, or what your heart is telling you, but the voice of reason tends to creep in. Your rational mind takes over and you start to ignore your intuition. It takes time and getting to know yourself, but eventually, you will find a balance between these two impulses. It's okay to be measured in your thinking, but try to make room for your intuition, too, as it may just be the thing that leads you down the right path.

I bet you know it right now: the thing you really want for yourself. You just pictured it, didn't you? You see, your gut instinct is always seeking the good things for your life, whether that's to go for that promotion, call that guy or take that trip.

It's our body's way of gently nudging us in the direction in which our heart truly lies. And it's your truth and yours alone, so follow it.

Self-doubt is the killer of dreams. Just when you convince yourself of something good, there it is. It's there in all of our big life choices, and even some small ones. It's there just when we thought we were doing okay, and it's there when we know we're not. We must come to see self-doubt in the same way we see hiccups: there is nothing really wrong, but they make us feel uncertain. The answer is not to roll up into a ball—just keep a clear head and try to breathe through it.

When faced with self-doubt, I write down a list of pros and cons. No matter what it is that I'm worried about, or what decision I'm trying to make, it helps me separate what is logical from what is overstated by my self-doubt. Try it, you'll see.

JEALOUSY

Jealousy is often just another expression of fear. It's another pesky emotion that scrambles our self-confidence and messes with our head. Luckily, it's possible to nip jealousy in the bud, but first, you have to recognise when you're feeling it.

Identifying jealousy can be tricky. Are you competing with that person or are you comparing yourself to that person? Neither is helpful, but the real problems start when you compare yourself to others. No two people have the same life—even identical twins—so you are going to find differences everywhere you look. Some people will have more, some will have less. Some people will be thinner, some will be larger. Being comfortable with where you fit among these variables is key.

Feeling jealous is a reflection of your dissatisfaction with something. It is rarely actually about the other person. For example, you might feel jealous if your friend has just bought a new car. It's not that you resent her for having it, but that you would like a new car yourself. The next time you're feeling jealous about something, turn the spotlight on yourself. Do you really want what she has? Or is there something lacking in your life? Instead of letting it drive you crazy, repeat to yourself that we have all felt like this, and try to let it go.

Three simple steps to reframe your attitude

1 CLARIFY YOUR FEELINGS. It's easy to be angry at yourself for feeling jealous and resentful, but try to unpack those emotions, reassure yourself that it's okay to feel this way and look at what you could improve in your own life.

2 LOOK BEYOND YOUR JEALOUSY. It's often those closest to us that we are jealous of, and the effects of jealousy can put these relationships under strain. Try to see your jealousy for what it is, and focus instead on the positive aspects of the relationship.

3 BE PROACTIVE. Take tangeable steps towards changing and improving your own life. The more you take control of the things you want to change, the better you will feel, and the less likely you will be to compare your life to others'.

A mindfulness method

Here is a simple mindfulness technique that I find hugely helpful to manage fear.

Find yourself a quiet spot where you won't be disturbed. Sit comfortably and close your eyes. Start by taking deep, steady breaths. Mentally scan your body and take note of where you feel any tension or tightness, then breathe deeply into those areas. Imagine what they look like, how much space they take up and what shape or colour they are. Get to know them intimately. Acknowledge that they are there, and try to accept that you cannot change them but you are safe. You are safe.

This exercise triggers your body's natural calm response. Give it a try whenever you are feeling anxious or overwhelmed.

Find your balance

STAY POSITIVE

Learning to be and stay positive is hard. Some people are pessimistic by nature and struggle to see the upside of things. But training yourself to see the positive in people and situations is worthwhile, as it offers you a different perspective and will save a lot of nervous energy.

I try to follow my son's lead with this. When something isn't going right, he says, 'Oh well'. Oh well. Just like that. When you think about it, it really is that simple. Some things go our way and some don't. At least we tried and we can try again, or simply move on: 'Oh well'.

HERE ARE A FEW STRATEGIES FOR LOOKING ON THE BRIGHT SIDE OF LIFE:

- **ASK YOURSELF REGULARLY: IS THIS A PRIORITY RIGHT NOW?** We often worry about minute things (or things that may or may not happen in the future). If the answer is no, let it go.
- **BEWARE OF 'SNOWBALL THINKING'.** Before a negative thought gains momentum, causing destruction and discontent, stop it in its tracks.
- **BE COMPASSIONATE.** Consider the victim of your negativity and be compassionate about their situation.
- **THINK OF IT AS CHANGING A MOOD.** Negative thinking is like a mood that has suddenly taken over. Do something to distract yourself and put yourself in a different mood.
- **LOOK FOR THE GOOD IN EVERY SITUATION.** Every. Single. Time. I've saved the best until last. This is the easiest way to become positive and happy. It sounds so ridiculously simple, but I credit this easy trick with being the foundation of all the positive changes in my life, including getting me through a marriage break-up. Always look for the silver lining. I promise, it is there.

Eleven lessons I wish I'd learned in my twenties

1 BE IN CHARGE OF YOUR MONEY—ALL OF IT. Understand where your money comes from and where it goes—even after you are married—and learn how to manage a budget. I can hear some of you saying, 'but I am not good with money, so my partner takes care of it'. I, too, used this excuse. I also never thought that I would be in a situation where I would need to care. Trust me and learn these skills.

2 LEARN HOW TO DO YOUR TAXES. Hire an accountant by all means, but make sure you understand every decision they make.

3 LEARN HOW TO DO ALL THE 'MAN'S' JOBS IN THE HOUSE. Whether it's changing a light bulb, fixing a fuse or changing a tyre: women are conditioned to believe that they can't do these things, but it's absolutely untrue. We are more than capable.

4 MAKE HEALTH YOUR NUMBER-ONE PRIORITY. If your body isn't functioning internally, it doesn't matter what you look like.

5 DON'T OVER-IDENTIFY WITH ANY ROLE; it's restrictive. Instead, express and enjoy your full character whenever you can.

6 ALLOW YOURSELF MORE TIME THAN YOU NEED TO COMPLETE A TASK. Never cram for deadlines or starve yourself to reach a weight-loss milestone just because you set yourself a date.

7 CUT YOURSELF SOME SLACK. You're probably doing better than you think you are.

8 BEWARE OF NEGATIVE SELF-TALK. Repeating 'I am so useless/fat/ugly/incapable' and so on is a complete waste of energy.

9 WORRY ABOUT YOURSELF. Try not to expend too much energy worrying about other people's lives. Remember, most people aren't worrying about you.

10 TRY NOT TO MAKE A BIG DEAL OUT OF THINGS. Repeat to yourself: this, too, shall pass. No matter how bad it is, don't overstate the facts.

11 NO MORE MAYBES. Every day is an opportunity to love yourself by committing to your health.

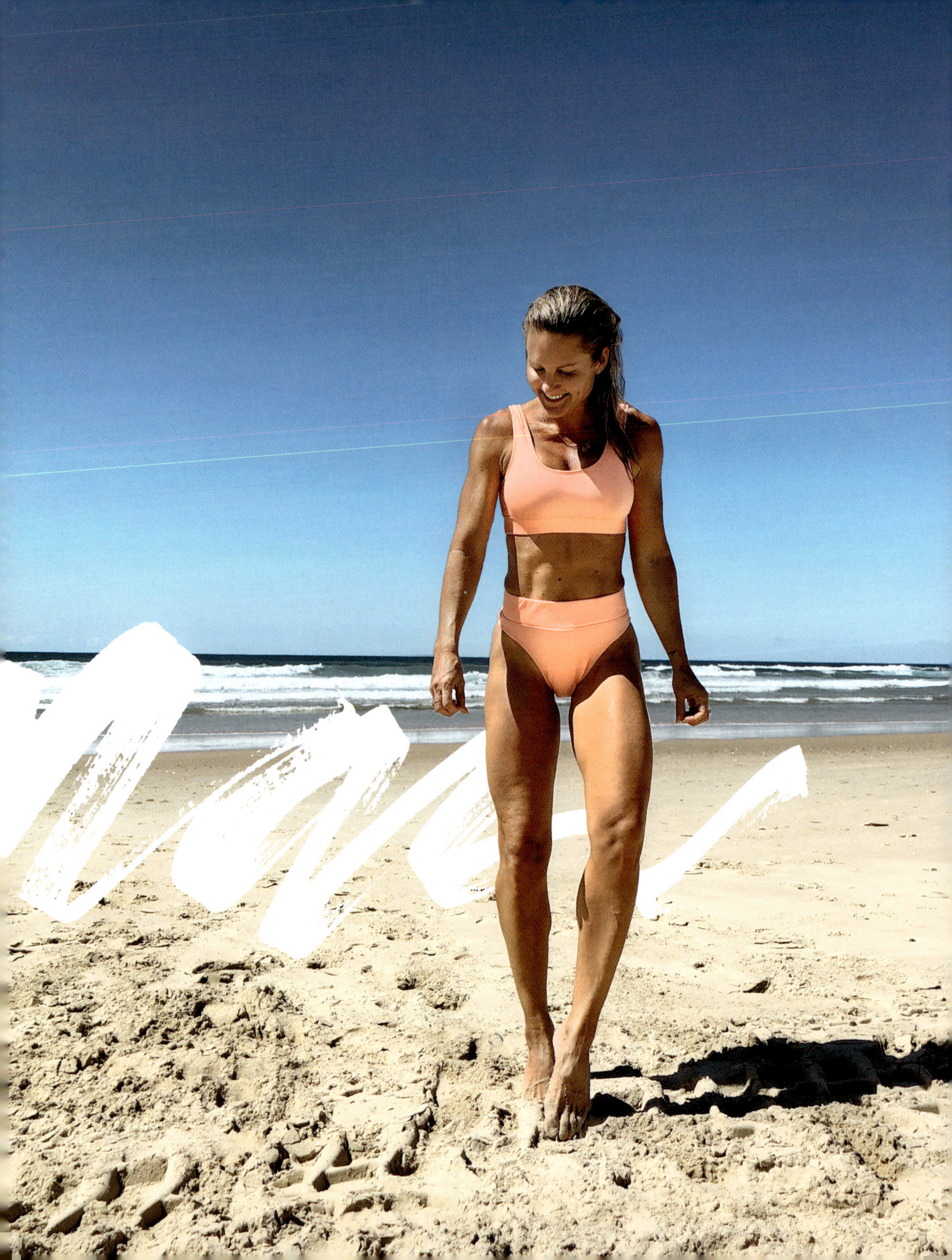

Own the emotional roller-coaster

The key to a happy, fulfilled life is to accept that, to a large degree, we can't control what happens. We let our emotions run amok and our stress rises to an unhealthy level, all because we believe that, if we try hard enough, we can control our destiny. Sure, you can control what you eat, how you live and the way you think but, for the most part, the things that happen in our lives are out of our hands.

To know true contentment, we have to make the decision to let it all go.

We need to stop blaming ourselves and others for the things that happen in our lives. Instead, look at what you can control and get really good at managing it.

As women, we almost enjoy complaining about things. We obsess over our lives, our partners, our careers, our children—everything. We pick apart what people say and try to guess at what they're thinking. We even invite our friends to overthink with us. They are there to listen, support us and make us feel better. Unfortunately, sometimes this isn't always the case, and it's important to identify these people before they make matters even worse.

TOXIC PEOPLE

We have all had at least one toxic person in our lives. Toxic people drain every bit of energy from you. They are energy vampires. Even worse, they consciously create conflict because they thrive on it.

Learning how to identify these people quickly is crucial. They are often people with no personal ambition; they take from you in every possible way. They generally view the world in a negative light, and they'll bring you down with them. In a way, I feel sorry for toxic people, as they are so deep into negative patterns of behaviour that there is little hope they will ever see the light. It's tempting to want to help them or 'fix' them, but the thing to remember is that most of these people will never change; they don't want to. The moment you identify one of these people, whether it's at work or among your group of friends, immediately restrict their access to your life and make it clear that you have set boundaries. This might mean removing them from your social media, or not giving them your phone number. Be proactive about it because, once you allow them into your life, you are vulnerable to their negativity.

Be independent

As women, and especially as mothers, we're often led to believe we don't have autonomy over our lives. That there are expectations on us and that we need to not only execute them, but execute them well.

Today, women have more opportunites than ever before. We can literally accomplish anything we choose to. We have career opportunities and financial stability and, on the whole, are no longer treated as the weaker sex. In many households, women are the main breadwinners. In my own family, my mum still works and my dad is retired.

In my own life, I am a single working mother, and I remind myself daily how proud I am to be able to do this. I was forced to stand on my own two feet in every way: emotionally, financially and physically. I learned a lot of new skills very quickly, and my personal strength grew inexorably. I am much more prepared for life than I ever was in my marriage, and that independence is so liberating.

> *Only when you are fully independent will you understand the meaning of true freedom.*

Only then will you know what it is to feel satisfaction and fulfilment, and the joy of not having to seek it from someone else. You and you alone are responsible for your happiness and whether or not you put it in the hands of another. Really seeing our value and loving ourselves for every inch of it is the only way to stand on our own two feet.

SEIZE YOUR OPPORTUNITIES

There is an extraordinary connection between taking opportunities to rest, to develop and to learn, and being happy, relaxed and satisfied. I am talking about the people who not only look for these opportunities, but who actually follow through on taking them. Sadly, many people don't.

It's easy to find excuses not to take for ourselves or seek change. In the workplace, we are almost discouraged from it. We're conditioned not to ask for a pay rise, speak up in meetings or go for promotions. As mothers, we're encouraged to stay home and look after our children instead of seeking career growth. Even as people, women are brought up to believe that they can't, and won't, have access to the same opportunities as men, so many of us don't even look for them.

However, when women realise that they are brave and worthy, a miraculous thing happens: they challenge themselves and everyone around them to have more, to be more, and to not be afraid to go after what they want. They speak their piece to their partner and negotiate more equal parenting. They ignore the misogyny at work and apply for that senior role. They start carving out the life they want, and improve their happiness in the process.

A common barrier to women seeking opportunities is that they feel the need to ask for permission. They feel the need to ask their superior if they should go for that job, or ask their partner if they can go out with their friends. But consider this: how often do you hear men asking? For anything? Men tell. They never seek permission. To be fair, this isn't necessarily their fault, for in the same way that girls were raised to be submissive, boys were encouraged to be obstinate.

> *You alone are responsible for your happiness*

THE TRAP OF MOTHERHOOD

Motherhood is beautiful, but it is also limiting. When I first became a mother, I felt like I couldn't leave the nest without feeling guilt: guilt for leaving my partner to cope and guilt for leaving my children. I also worried about what I could come home to. Would it all fall apart when I left? Often, something would get broken or I'd get a phone call to say 'I can't fix X, Y or Z', or to ask 'how do you do this again?' Suddenly, my husband wouldn't be able to cope. It baffles me how some partners become inept at performing basic tasks right when they ought to be the most responsible. Is it to ensure that they aren't left holding the baby again? I hope not.

In the early stages of motherhood, women tend to be in control of the baby, with their partners doing the occasional nappy change or bottle-feed. But we really need to let up. We need to say, 'this baby is yours, too', and actually feel okay about relinquishing some responsibility.

> **Same-sex parents aren't restricted by gender roles. They share the work and overcome the challenges together, and there is a lot we can learn from them.**

I get it, having kids is a big deal, and can be pretty scary, but it's just as new and frightening for a new mum as it is for a new dad. We should be in it together, and we should encourage our partner to take breaks and time out to feel rested and refreshed.

LEADING LADY, NOT SUPERWOMAN

Women have a habit of trying to be superwomen: trying to juggle everything. People say it to me all the time: 'you're a supermum' or 'you are a superwoman'. While these people are trying to pay me a compliment, it's actually not helpful. I have never tried to be super anything. It doesn't all happen by magic; I work my arse off. I set myself a goal and work and work until I achieve it. I'm pretty sure I got my strong work ethic from my mum and my much-adored grandma (my mum's mum). Both of these strong women are the living embodiment of hard work. They taught me that sitting around waiting for things to happen is a waste of time; we have to go out there and make them happen. It's not about being a superwoman, but a leading lady in your own life.

I prefer the idea of a leading lady to a superwoman. It is more realistic and emphasises a woman's agency and hard work. A leading lady sets her goals and goes about achieving them with dignity and focus. She walks with purpose down her chosen path, carrying her children carefully with her. She is honest, caring and respected. She knows when to say no and doesn't feel guilty for doing so. She knows when to work hard and when to take a break. This type of woman is in all of us, we just have to find her. When we look to become her, we discover the very best version of ourselves.

In contrast, the superwoman thinks she can do everything and be there for everyone, always. She never says no. She can't set boundaries, and she scrambles to juggle more than she can manage. She is concerned with keeping up appearances and being accepted by everyone she meets. She never aspires to be an individual. Superwoman might be good at spinning plates, but at what cost? Her health? Her children? Her marriage? Something has to give, and we should never feel guilty or embarrassed about asking for help.

A leading lady sets and achieves her goals

Find your balance 113

6

Fit Mama fitness

TIME TO STEP UP

As a new mother, making time to exercise can be hard, but it is imperative that you keep fit and healthy in order to nourish both yourself and your baby.

Women require high-intensity, quality speed-weight sessions to maintain lean muscle. The Fit Mama program is designed for every body type and ability level. My fitness systems concentrate on quality over quantity, delivering targeted movements to create a lean, well-aligned and beautiful body.

I HAVE CREATED TWO SEVEN-DAY FITNESS PLANS THAT CAN BE USED THROUGHOUT THE YEAR.

The **Steady Fit program** is for those who have less time to devote to their fitness, or need a flexible fitness schedule, so it is spread out over two weeks instead of one. It focuses on a more gradual progression, with sets that target particular problem areas for women, such as the bum and thighs. It is great for beginners or for anyone wanting to rebuild their fitness after a long break.

The **Fast Fit program** is a high-intensity program for women who are prepared to put in the hard work every day to see quick results. It contains seven different sets for the seven days of the week, each based on HIIT techniques to target specific muscle groups and achieve results in a short period of time.

Both programs will produce the same result; it is just a matter of personal preference. Once you get used to the different sets, try mixing them up to keep it interesting.

I recommend starting with the Steady Fit program for one month before progressing to the Fast Fit program. After two months, I recommend adding in the gym bonus set (Set 7) to give you a bit more variety. This bonus set is great for keeping the body guessing and throwing a curveball in every now and then. This is more productive for weight loss than simply repeating the same exercise program over and over again.

Keep fit to nourish your body and your mind

After three months of the Fit Mama program, you can continue with your favourite combination workouts or, week by week, alternate between Steady Fit and Fast Fit. Personally, I complete Steady Fit and Fast Fit on alternative weeks and have done so for many years, as I find this the most effective way to keep in shape.

You can complete these sets any time of the day. However, I find it most beneficial to complete my cardio first thing in the morning, followed by a set late in the afternoon or in the evening.

The nine worst gym habits hindering weight loss

One question I am regularly asked by clients is what are they doing wrong in the gym. In order to see the results of all your hard work, make sure that you don't fall into these habits:

1. Spending time on your phone while on the treadmill
2. Not working hard enough on the bike
3. Taking too long a rest between sets
4. Working too slowly
5. Using weights that are too heavy
6. Dropping weights
7. Spending too much time on fixed-weight machines and not enough on free weights
8. Losing your form during exercises
9. Not completing a workout or taking short cuts

Fit Mama fitness

Tips for completing Fit Mama workouts

☆ Before starting the Fit Mama program, make sure you consult with your doctor or health professional about any pre-existing health conditions or injuries.

☆ Before you start a workout, make sure you warm up properly with stretches (see the Fit ball and foam roller stretch set, page 132) and gentle exercises that slowly increase your heart rate, such as jogging on the spot. This will help you to avoid injury.

☆ During each workout, concentrate on maintaining your form to avoid injuries. If you're not sure how to complete a certain exercise or movement, take a look at the Exercises guide (see pages 120–133) or ask a gym instructor to demonstrate.

☆ After every workout, complete a cooldown of stretches and gentle movements to gradually bring your heart rate back down and ensure that your muscles do not seize up.

Equipment

If you are planning to work out at home or have a lovely outdoor workout space, you will need the following equipment:

- 2 x 5–7.5 kg dumbbells (or 2 x 2-litre bottles of water)
- 1 x 7 kg medicine ball (or 1 x 7.5 kg dumbbell)
- Workout bench (or sturdy chair)
- Fitness ball
- Gym or yoga mat
- Foam roller

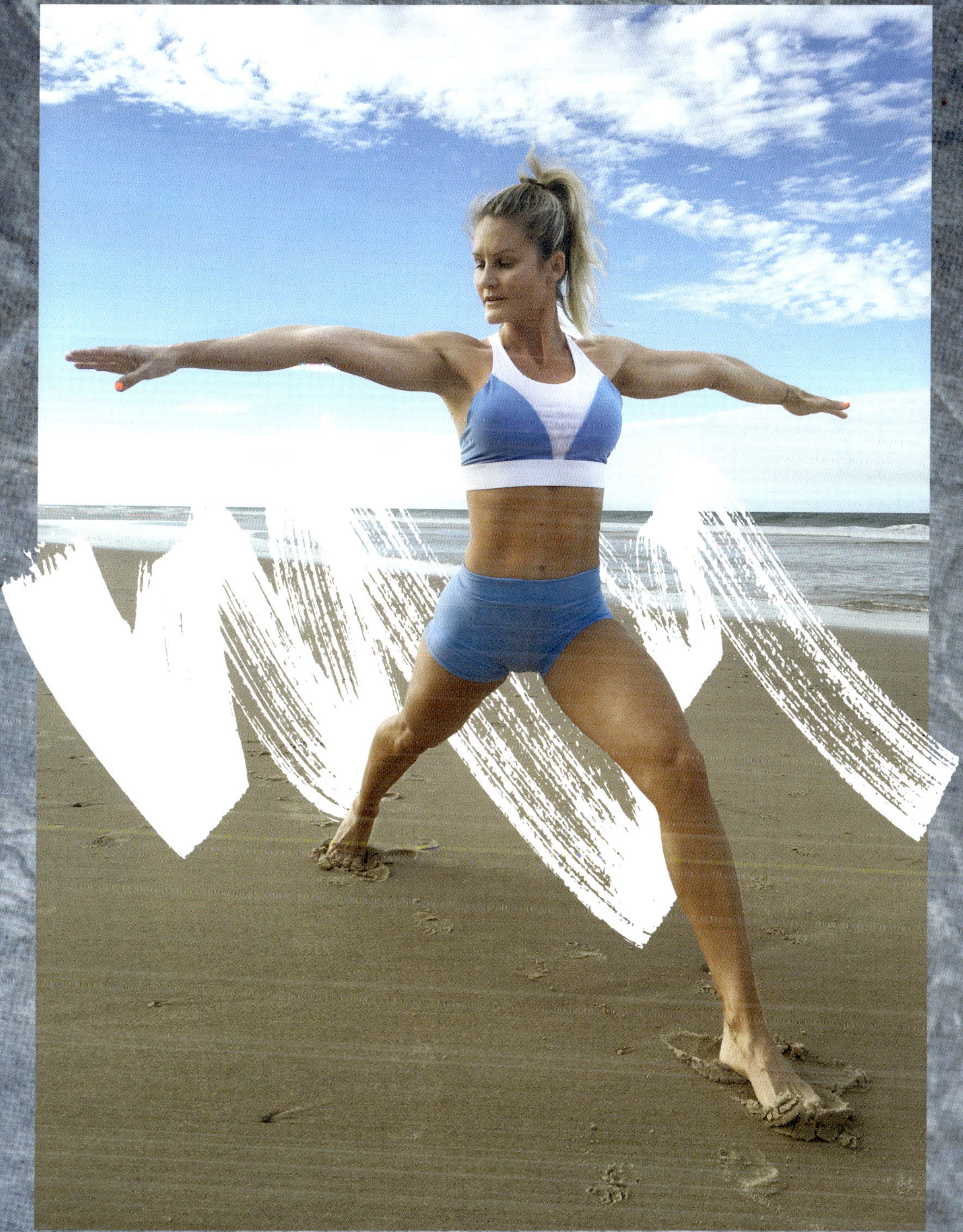

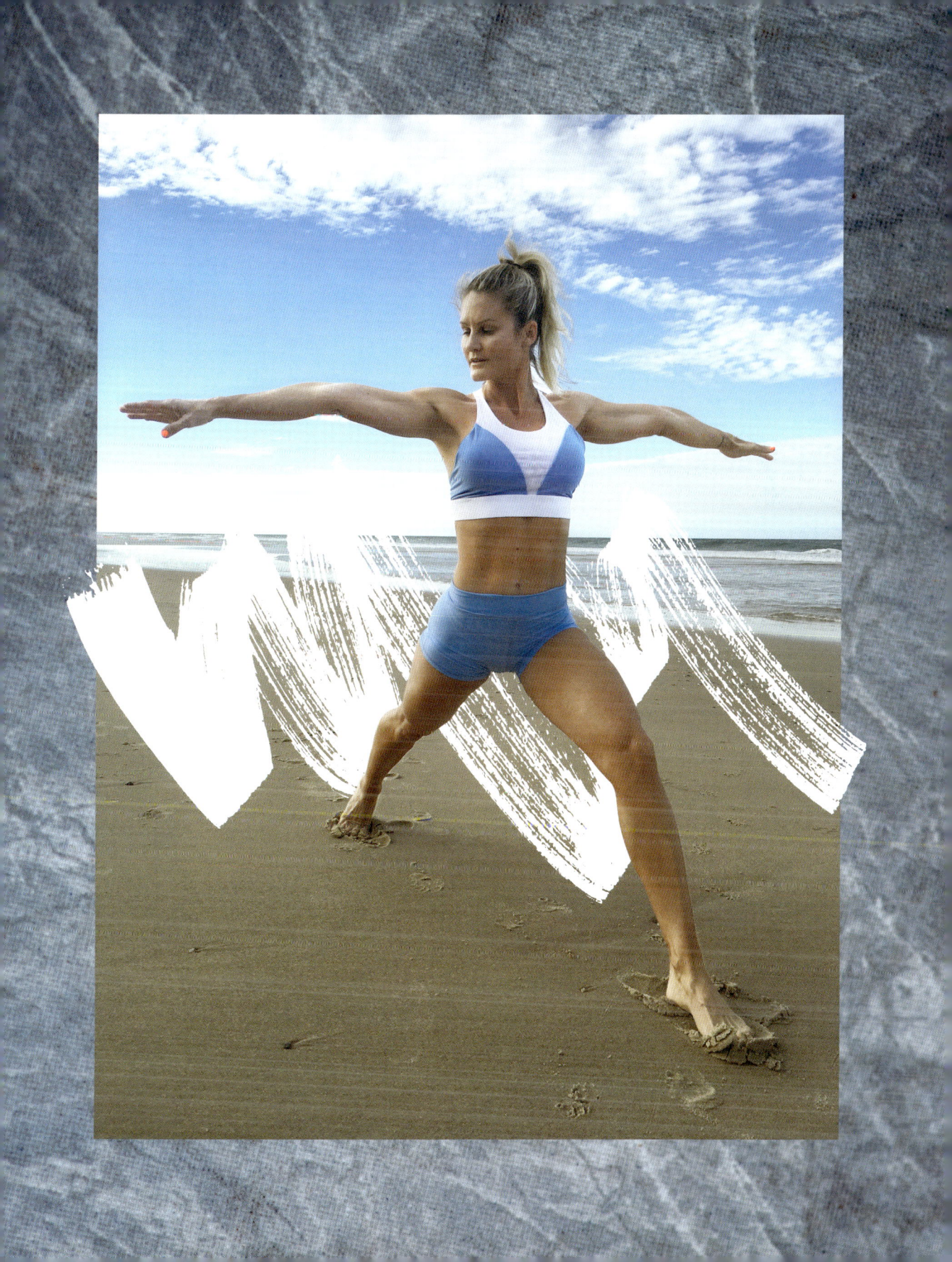

Exercises guide

Most people know what a squat or a push-up is, but what about the other movements?

Lunges

CURTSY LUNGE

STEP-BACK LUNGE

Step one leg behind the other and lower into a deep lunge with your knee just touching the ground. Come back up and repeat on the other side.

Raise your left knee, then step your left foot backwards into a lunge with your knee just touching the ground. Come back up and repeat on the other side.

JUMP LUNGE

Step one leg forwards and lower into a lunge with your knee just touching the ground. Bring your bent knee forwards into a jump, then swap sides.

SIDE LUNGE

Take a wide stance. Bend one knee towards the ground. Return to a standing position and repeat on the other side. Add weights if desired.

BARBELL LUNGE *Gym*

Place a barbell on your shoulders and tuck in your elbows. Step one foot forwards into a lunge, then return to a standing position. Repeat on the other side.

WALKING LUNGE

Step one leg forwards and lower into a lunge with your opposite knee just touching the ground. Repeat on the other side and continue 'walking' in the lunge position for about 10 metres.

Fit Mama fitness

Squats

SPLIT SQUAT

Place one foot behind you on a bench, box or chair. Straighten your arms in front of you to help you get your balance. Activate your core and roll your shoulders back. Drop your stabilising knee towards the ground, moving your hands to your hips, then come back up in a controlled movement.

SIDE-TO-SIDE SQUAT JUMP

Stand with your feet shoulder width apart. Lower yourself into a squat position, then jump from side to side.

122 Fit Mama

DEEP BOOTY SQUAT

Take a wide stance with your legs apart. Squat, in one controlled movement, until your knees are about 45 degrees to the floor. Slowly come back up. Keep your arms outstretched for stability.

SUMO SQUAT

Take a wide stance with your legs apart. Holding a dumbbell between your legs, lower into a deep squat and pause briefly. Slowly come back up. Repeat.

SQUAT JUMP

Lower into a squat position. Jump upwards in one explosive motion. Land, returning your body to a squat position. Keep your hands clasped in front of you for balance.

BARBELL SQUAT *Gym*

Place a barbell on your shoulders and tuck in your elbows. Lower into a squat position. Slowly come back up.

BARBELL HACK SQUAT *Gym*

Adjust the machine to ensure your back fits firmly against the pads. Allow the machine to guide you in a squat. Push back up.

Taps & raises

WIDE-LEG WEIGHT TAP

Take a wide stance. Lower down on one side and tap the ground close to your foot, then return to a standing position. Repeat on the other side. Use a pair of light dumbbells if desired.

PLANK TAP

Begin in the plank position. Raising your hips towards the sky, reach down and tap your opposite thigh. Repeat on the other side.

TOE-TAP CRUNCH

Lie on your back on a mat with your legs together and extended upwards. Raise your arms upwards and tap your toes in an abdominal crunch. Add weights if desired.

TOE-TAP LEG RAISE

Lie on a mat with your legs outstretched. Raise your arms above your head in a diving position. Raise one leg towards the sky and reach your hands towards your foot. Hover your other leg just off the mat. Repeat.

BICEP CURL WITH OVERHEAD PRESS

From a standing position holding dumbbells, curl the dumbbells up. Pause here, then raise the dumbbells up over your head, twisting the dumbbells to face the opposite direction. Lower down, then repeat.

Fit Mama fitness 125

Walkouts

WALKOUT

CATERPILLAR WALKOUT

From a standing position, bend your upper body forwards and walk your hands along the ground (bend your knees slightly) into a push-up position. Pause, then walk yourself back up. Repeat.

Holding light dumbbells, walk your hands along the ground into a plank position, then slowly walk your feet forwards as you move across the ground.

Push-ups

STANDING-PRESS PUSH-UP

Holding a pair of light dumbbells, begin in a plank position. Lower into a push-up, return to a plank position, then jump your feet forwards and stand, holding the weights at your side. Repeat.

Push-ups

PUSH-UP CLIMBER

Complete a push-up. From the plank position at the end of the push-up, alternate bringing each knee to the space in between your elbows at a fast pace. Finish with another push-up.

PUSH-UP JUMP

Place your hands on a mat, shoulder width apart. Jump your feet backwards into a plank position. Lower into a push-up, then jump your feet forwards and stand up. Repeat.

Other

PUSH-UP DEADLIFT PRESS

1

2

3

Complete a push-up with or without dumbbells. Jump your feet forwards and stand up. Raise the dumbbells (if using) into a bicep curl, then press them overhead. Return the weights to the ground and repeat.

V SIT-UP

1

Lie on a mat with your legs outstretched and your arms over your head in a diving position. Bring your legs, arms and shoulders upwards simultaneously, and meet them in the middle to create an inverted V shape. Lower them back down.

T-STABILISATION

1

From a plank position, raise one arm straight up towards the ceiling, stacking one foot on top of the other. Hold for five seconds. Repeat on the other side.

Fit Mama fitness 129

Other

CATERPILLAR PLANK-ROW SLIDE

Begin in a push-up position. Twisting on your toes, slowly pull one arm back in a row. Return your hand to the ground and repeat on the other side. You should creep forwards as you do this exercise.

SUPERMAN

Lying on your stomach, raise both arms, both legs and your chest off the floor (as if you were skydiving) and hold for five seconds. Slowly lower back down in a controlled movement.

BENCH DIP

Sit on a bench with your hands beside your thighs. Move your bottom forwards off the bench and dip down towards the ground. Push on your hands to raise yourself back up, then repeat. Extend your legs to make it harder, or bend them to make it easier.

FLUTTER KICKS

Lie on your mat with your arms by your sides. raise both your legs slightly, held tightly together, then flutter your feet in little kicks. Don't let your heels touch the ground.

LYING KNEE RAISE

Lie on your back on a mat with your legs outstretched. Raise one bent knee towards your chest. Use your hand to move the knee in a circular motion, crunching towards the knee. Repeat on the other side.

STEP-UPS

Stand in front of a bench and step one foot up. Hold for a few seconds, keeping your other leg straight, then lower down and repeat on the other side.

Fit Mama fitness

Fit ball and foam roller stretch set

DOWNWARD-FACING DOG/ ENERGY STRETCH

Begin on your hands and knees. On an inhale, come up onto your toes, then, on an exhale, lift your hips up towards the sky into an upside-down V shape. Spread your fingers wide and gradually work towards bringing your heels to the ground. Hold for four or five breaths, then relax.

PIGEON STRETCH

Starting in a push-up position, bring your right knee forwards and keep your left leg straight. Place your left hand behind you on the mat. Gently lower yourself onto the right hip, resting on the knee. Hold for 20 seconds. Swap sides and repeat four times.

UPWARD-FACING DOG/ ENERGY STRETCH

Lie on your stomach on a mat. Place your hands beside your shoulders. In one movement, raise your head up towards the sky, lifting your thighs and knees off the mat. Hold for five seconds, then come down. Repeat.

SEATED GROIN AND PIGEON TWIST

Sit on a mat with your legs outstretched. Bend your right knee and tuck your left leg, also bent, underneath. Place your right hand behind you on the mat and slowly twist your torso. Push your right knee gently with your left hand to deepen the stretch.

QUAD ROLL

Lie on your stomach on a mat and tuck a foam roller underneath your quads. Come up onto your hands and gently roll your quads back and forth across the roller.

HAMSTRING ROLL

Sit on a mat with your legs outstretched. Working one leg at a time, tuck a foam roller underneath your hamstring. Come up onto your fingers and gently roll your hamstring back and forth across the roller.

SHOULDER ROLL

Place a foam roller at about shoulder height on a mat. Sit in front of the roller and lean back to rest your shoulders on it. Lift your bottom off the floor and gently roll your shoulders back and forth across the roller.

FOAM ROLLER CHEST/ SPINE STRETCH

Place a foam roller vertically on the floor. Carefully lay over it, so that one end of the roller supports your tailbone and the other end supports your head. Let your arms fall to the sides, opening out your chest. Gently roll from side to side, massaging the spine.

ITB-BAND RELEASE

Sit on a mat with your legs outstretched. Tuck a foam roller under your bottom, then gently turn onto your left side, straightening your left leg and bending your right knee over your left leg to steady yourself. Roll back and forth gently. Repeat on the other side.

Picture page 142

Fit Mama fitness 133

Let's get fit!

You've gathered your equipment, found the perfect spot to work out uninterrupted, and you're feeling pumped. Time to get started. On the following pages are weekly workouts for both Fit Mama Steady Fit and Fit Mama Fast Fit. Depending on where you are in your fitness journey, select one of the two.

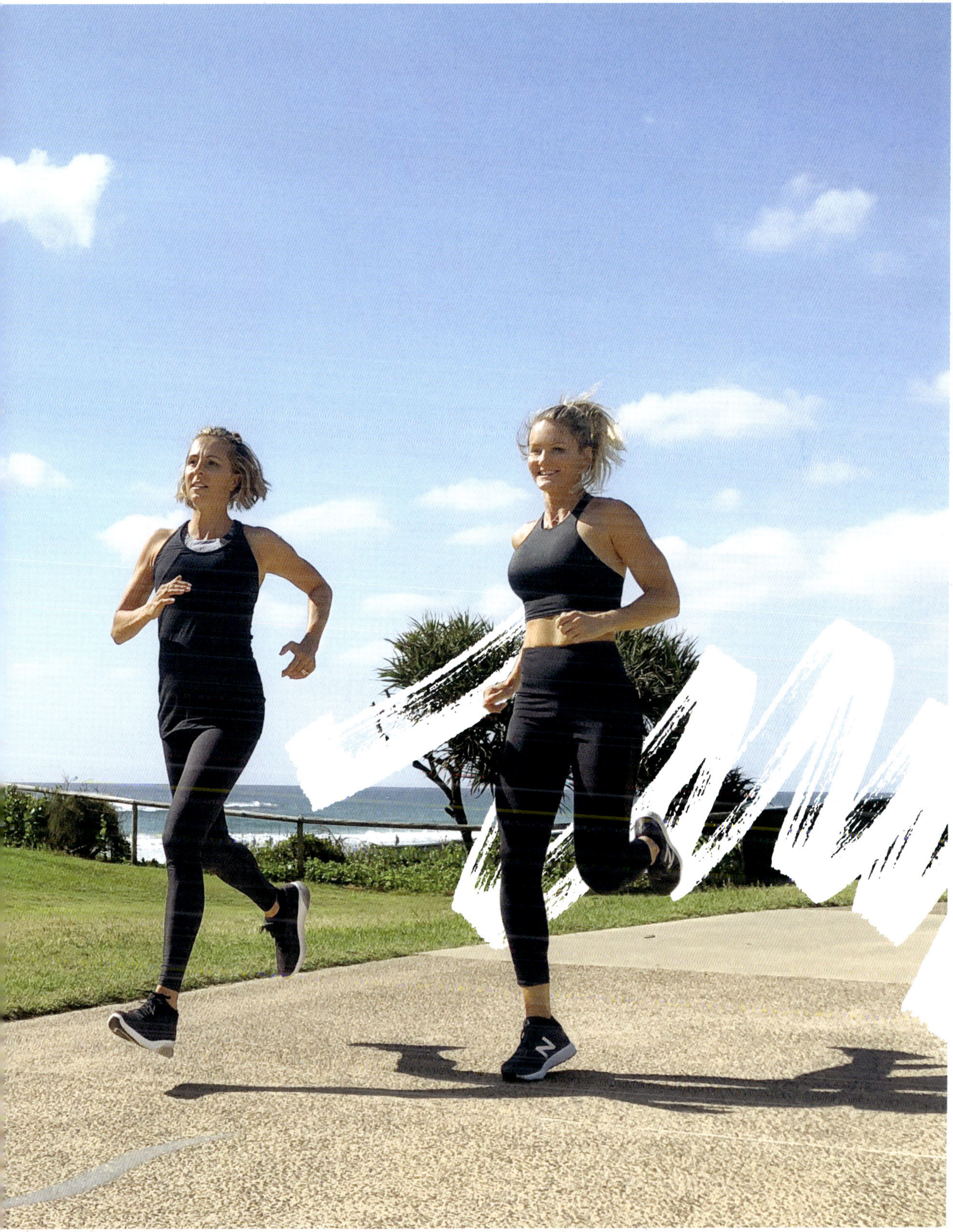

Fit Mama Steady Fit: Week One

TRAINING SESSIONS	AM	PM
Monday	30-minute walk	Rest
Tuesday	30-minute walk; 2 minutes fast walk, 1 minute slow	SET 1: Full-body boost (page 140)
Wednesday	SET 2: Quick energy boost (page 140)	Rest
Thursday	30-minute walk	SET 3: Speed ladder grit set (page 140)
Friday	30-minute walk; 2 minutes fast walk, 1 minute slow	Rest
Saturday	30-minute walk	SET 4: Core workout (page 140)
Sunday	Long walk	Rest

Fit Mama Steady Fit: Week Two

TRAINING SESSIONS	AM	PM
Monday	30-minute walk	SET 5: Upper-body burner (page 141)
Tuesday	30-minute walk; 2 minutes fast walk, 1 minute slow	Rest
Wednesday	30-minute walk	SET 6: Whole-body reshape (page 141)
Thursday	SET 8: Speed set (page 142)	Rest
Friday	30-minute walk; 2 minutes fast walk, 1 minute slow	SET 9: Booty lifter (page 142)
Saturday	30-minute walk	Rest
Sunday	Long walk	SET 10: Fit ball and foam roller stretch set (page 142)

Fit Mama fitness

Get moving!

Fit Mama Fast Fit: Weekly program

TRAINING SESSIONS	AM	PM
Monday	30-minute walk	SET 1: Full-body boost (page 140)
Tuesday	20-minute run with 5-minute walk at the beginning and end	SET 4: Core workout (page 140)
Wednesday	30 minutes speed cardio, such as running intervals **OR** SET 2: Quick energy boost (page 140)	Rest
Thursday	30-minute walk	SET 6: Whole-body reshape (page 141) **OR** SET 9: Booty lifter (page 142)
Friday	15-minute run **AND** SET 5: Upper-body burner (page 141)	SET 10: Fit ball and foam roller stretch set (page 142)
Saturday	30-minute walk	SET 8: Speed set (page 142)
Sunday	Long walk	Rest

Fit Mama fitness

Set 1: Full-body boost

TIME: 30 minutes
REPETITIONS: 3–5

Warm up

- 10 x push-ups
- 1 minute of jump lunges
- 10 x split squats
- 1 minute of squats (hands clasped in front)
- 10 x toe-tap leg raises
- 1 minute of side-to-side squat jumps
- 10 x walkouts

Stretch and cool down

Set 2: Quick energy boost

TIME: 20 minutes
REPETITIONS: 3

Warm up

- 10 x squats
- 1 minute of push-up jumps
- 10 x side lunges
- 1 minute of push-up jumps
- 10 x curtsy lunges
- 1 minute of push-up jumps
- 10 walkouts

Stretch and cool down

Set 3: Speed ladder grit set

TIME: 40 minutes
REPETITIONS: 3

Warm up

- 10 x push-ups
- 12 x step-back lunges
- 2 minutes of squat jumps
- 16 x bridges with knee in climber position
- 2 minutes of squat jumps
- 20 x walkouts
- 2-minute skip, run or walk

Stretch and cool down

Set 4: Core workout

TIME: 30 minutes
REPETITIONS: 3

Warm up

- 20 x plank taps
- 10 x side-to-side squat jumps
- 20 x V sit-ups
- 10 x squat jumps
- 20 x flutter kicks
- 10 x forward lunges
- 20 x lying knee raises
- 30-second T-stabilisation
- 30-second Superman

Stretch and cool down

Set 5: Upper-body burner

TIME: 30 minutes
REPETITIONS: 4–6

Warm up

> 10 x caterpillar walkouts with a 5-second hold in plank position
> 10 x push-ups with a 30-second hold in push-up or bridge position
> 30 seconds of rest
> 10 x plank taps with a 30-second hold in bridge position
> 1 minute of bicycle crunches
> 30 seconds of rest
> 10 x caterpillar walkouts with a 5-second hold in plank position
> 10 x bench dips

Stretch and cool down

Set 6: Whole-body reshape

TIME: 40 minutes
REPETITIONS: 3

Warm up

> 20 x step-ups
> 10 x split squats
> 10 x deep booty squats
> 20 x walking lunges
> 10 x standing-press push-ups
> 10 x bicep curls with overhead press (5 kg weights)
> 20 x toe-tap crunches with weights
> 2-minute fast run, stepper or cycle

Stretch and cool down

Gym Bonus set

This is a session I use on rainy days when the weather is bad and I prefer to work out in the gym. I also like to use it when I'm feeling bored with the rest of the sets. It adds variety and keeps your body guessing.

Set 7: Leg-shaper

TIME: 45 minutes
REPETITIONS: 3

20-minute fast-walk warm-up

> 10–12 leg extensions (on machine; 20 kg single leg)
> 10–12 leg extensions (on machine; 35 kg both legs)
> 20 x side-to-side squat jumps
> 10–12 x 20 kg barbell lunges
> 10–12 x 20 kg barbell squats
> 20 x jump lunges
> 10–12 barbell hack squats (hold at a 45-degree angle)
> 10–12 single-leg press (30 kg)
> 10–12 double-leg press (60–70 kg)
> 1-minute speed-cycle

Stretch and cool down

Fit Mama fitness

Set 8: Speed set

TIME: 40 minutes
REPETITIONS: 3

20-minute warm-up run or walk

> 16 x walking lunges
> 15 x push-up deadlift press combos
> 14 x caterpillar plank-row slides
> 13 x toe-tap crunches
> 12 x side-to-side squat jumps
> 11 x toe-tap crunches and foot scoops
> 10 x split squats
> 1–2 minute run or cycle between each repetition

Stretch and cool down

Set 9: Booty lifter

TIME: 45 minutes
REPETITIONS: 3

20-minute warm-up run, cycle or walk

> 10 x bicep curls with overhead press
> 10 x sumo squats
> 10 x high-knee speed steps
> 10 x high-knee step-back lunges
> 10 x squats with 5–8 kg dumbbell press
> 10 x wide-leg weight taps
> 10 x push-up climbers
> 10-second plank
> 10 x speed sit-ups

Stretch and cool down

ITB-band release, description on page 133

Set 10: Fit ball and foam roller stretch set

To safeguard your body from injury, it is important to stretch after each workout. This stretch set should only take five minutes, but it will ensure that you are lengthening your muscles and helping them flush out the lactic acid that builds up during training. For the extended set, see pages 132–3.

Live the ambition; it's your mission

7

Fit Mama Fuel

HEALTHY RECIPES FOR BUSY FAMILIES

The way we choose to fuel our bodies is our most basic act of love and appreciation for our health. Good nutrition is integral to a successful fitness program, as no amount of exercise will burn off poor-quality junk food. Establishing a healthy relationship with food, and accepting that food and fitness go hand in hand, is imperative to success.

In the Fit Mama program, calorie counting is not encouraged, as it can lead to obsessive behaviour; however, educating yourself about food and the function of calories will arm you with the information you need to make the right food choices.

The Fit Mama fuel regime suggests eating six small meals a day. Eating little and often is proven to increase metabolic rate and help you burn fuel more efficiently. It also helps to curb hunger and keep you feeling satiated and less likely to turn to junk food.

WEIGHT-LOSS PROMOTERS

These foods contain valuable minerals and vitamins that are essential to fat loss. They also help to keep you feeling full, which will prevent overeating. Make sure you always have a good supply of these ingredients on hand.

- Chicken and turkey
- White fish
- Seafood
- Eggs
- Feta, mozzarella and goat's cheese
- Almonds and walnuts
- Sesame seeds and pepitas (pumpkin seeds)
- Black and cannellini beans
- Olives
- Seaweed
- Broccoli, ginger, spinach, bok choy (pak choy), kale, lettuce, flat-leaf (Italian) parsley, capsicum (pepper), sweet potato, pumpkin and turnip
- Bananas, blueberries, cherries, figs, guava, mango, apple, pineapple, apricots, lemons, limes, plums, prunes, dates, strawberries and watermelon

Tips for staying on a healthy food budget

1 EAT FRESH, SEASONAL FOODS. Look for fruits and vegetables that are on special, as these tend to be the ones in season. And don't worry if your favourite berry is a lot more expensive in the winter than it was in the summer; I buy fresh blueberries when they are on special, and use frozen blueberries when they're not. I also use grated apple as an alternative to blueberries, as apples are much cheaper.

2 BUY LOCAL WHENEVER POSSIBLE. I visit organic markets near closing time, grab some of their specials and think up recipes to use unusual foods. Buying local also reduces food miles and supports local producers.

3 REDUCE YOUR PORTION SIZES. Eating large portions of food inevitably leads to waste, which is just money down the drain.

4 PREPARE FOOD THOUGHTFULLY. I make my own muesli and buy nuts and seeds on special or in bulk. I store the muesli in a container for the week.

5 BUY IN BULK. I buy salmon fillets in bulk and cook them up on Sunday night for the week ahead, ready for adding to a breakfast omelette, on top of a salad for lunch for work, or as an easy dinner with vegies after meetings or kids' sport.

6 USE THE FREEZER. The freezer is your friend. Think: lots of frozen fruit, portioned-up pesto for using on salmon or fish, or even nut slice for snacks. Stick any overripe bananas in there, too, and use them for fresh fruit smoothies. Just remember to peel them first.

7 GROW YOUR OWN. This is one of the easiest—and most satisfying—ways to make sure you're getting the freshest produce. We grow our own herbs and limes, and it's much cheaper than buying them in the supermarket.

Fit Mama fuel

Planning Fit Mama meals

On the Fit Mama program, I recommend that people consume six small meals a day. The cheat sheets below and on page 150 give options for each of the six meals. Select one option for each meal, and always remember to drink plenty of water at each mealtime.

Meal 1: Breakfast options

- Fave Smoothie (page 170) or any smoothie that you like
- 2 boiled eggs, 1 piece of toast, salt and pepper
- Warm porridge with sliced banana and a sprinkle of coconut sugar
- Porridge with fresh blueberries and almond milk or milk of your choice
- 2 fried eggs with fresh spinach, cherry tomatoes, salt and pepper
- 1 piece of toast with avocado and spinach or chicken breast and tomato
- Muesli (page 157) with yoghurt and fruit
- To accompany any option above: coffee with almond milk (or milk of your choice) or green tea

For my favourite breakfast recipes, see pages 152–7.

Meal 2: Morning tea options

- Bircher muesli with grated apple
- 10–12 dry-roasted almonds and a small coffee with no sugar
- 2 rice cakes with peanut butter and sliced banana
- 2 rice cakes with tuna, tomato and spinach
- Smoothie of your choice (page 170)
- 1 square of Energy Slice (page 156)

For my go-to morning tea and snack recipes, see pages 166–75.

Coffee

It is imperative that you have your last coffee of the day mid-morning. If you crave warm drinks after that, swap coffee for green tea or warm water with lemon.

Dinner leftovers can make healthy, filling lunches

Meal 3: Lunch options

- Salad with chicken breast (add roasted beetroot, grated apple or pear, seeds or crushed, dry-roasted almonds for extra flavour)
- Mashed vegetables with grilled or baked chicken breast
- Homemade vegetable soup
- Roasted vegetables with fresh steamed broccoli
- Baked tofu and salad
- Leftover dinner from the night before

For simple and delicious lunch recipes, see pages 158–65.

Meal 4: Afternoon snack options

- Protein shake (preferably a chocolate flavoured protein to eliminate those 3 pm sugar cravings)
- Rice cakes with peanut butter and sliced banana
- Smoothie of your choice (page 170)
- 1 square of Energy Slice (page 156)
- Handful of almonds
- ½ cup edamame beans
- 4 rye crackers with hummus
- 1 carrot or 1 celery stick with nut butter

For fast and filling afternoon snack recipes, see pages 166–75.

Sugar

To avoid the late afternoon slump, introduce an element of sweetness to your afternoon snack. Try a smoothie or flavoured protein shake.

Fit Mama fuel 149

Meal 5: Dinner options

Dinners are meant to be organised without being strict. Below is a list of suggestions for protein, vegetables, carbohydrates and fats. Select one item from each list to create a meal.

- 1 portion of protein: chicken, turkey, lean red meat, fish or plant-based protein such as tofu or tempeh
- 1 portion of steamed, roasted or mashed vegetables
- 1 portion of carbohydrate: ½ cup brown rice, ½ cup quinoa with chia seeds or ½ of a roasted sweet potato
- Small portion of fat: olive oil, avocado, nuts or seeds

For my family's favourite dinner recipes, see pages 176–85.

Planning

Planning your dinners is a great way to help you stick to a meal plan for the week. Buy only what you need to make your chosen dinners, and make sure you stick to them.

Dairy-free Mango Gelato
(recipe page 201)

Meal 6: Dessert options

- Smoothie of your choice (page 170)
- Handful of blueberries
- Handful of sliced strawberries
- 1 apple, sliced
- To accompany any option above: relaxing chamomile tea
- Something a little more indulgent (see below)

For decadent yet surprisingly healthy dessert recipes, see pages 186–203.

Muesli
(recipe page 157)

Chocolate Protein Balls
(recipe page 169)

Apricot Cashew Protein Balls
(recipe page 169)

FOOD STAPLES

To avoid boredom, and to ensure that you eat a variety of foods that everyone in the family will enjoy, make sure you vary what you cook each week. Having said that, I find it helpful to stick to some basic staples to get me through the week, such as **Mashed Vegetables** (which go with everything; page 185), a big batch of **Muesli** (page 157) and some **Heavenly Hummus** (page 175), which keeps well in the fridge for three to four days and is great for snacking with rice cakes or carrot and celery sticks.

At least once a fortnight, I make an **Energy Slice** (page 156), which is great for school lunchboxes or work snacks. The same goes for a **Picnic Pie** (page 160), which is a fun way to get kids eating more vegies.

With so many protein and bliss ball combinations to choose from (truly, you're only limited by your imagination), it's easy to get variety in there. A couple of my favourites are the **Chocolate Protein Balls** (page 169) and **Apricot Cashew Protein Balls** (page 169). You can make these in advance and freeze them, too. A loaf of **Wholegrain Bread** (page 174) also goes down well at any time of the day.

Taking the time to prepare some staple items for the week, fortnight or month will ease some strain during a busy working week and ensure that you don't fall victim to temptation.

Fit Mama fuel

BREAKFAST

Breakfast is still the most important meal of the day, as our body needs a good hit of nutrients to get going. Primarily, it boosts metabolic rate and increases fat loss. As part of the Fit Mama program, breakfast must be eaten before 8 am; any later and you risk breakfast slipping into lunch, or becoming too hungry and feeling the need to snack. Eating too late in the morning also puts the body into starvation mode, meaning that anything you do eat is more likely to be stored as fat. Skipping breakfast is not an option, as it ultimately leads to binge eating and weight gain.

If you struggle to eat early, try getting up a little bit earlier and enjoying a cup of warm water, tea or coffee to stimulate your stomach. Slowly introduce the habit of eating earlier, and chew your food slowly and thoroughly, allowing a new neural pathway to form.

Spiced Vanilla Banana Smoothie

(recipe page 157)

Energy Slice

(recipe page 156)

These juices are great for first thing in the morning to stimulate your stomach and give a quick burst of clean energy. They also work as snacks, and are easy to prepare ahead and take with you.

To make these juices, you will need a hand-held blender or a high-speed blender. Simply combine the ingredients in the blender and blitz until smooth.

BELLY BALANCER

Serves 1

125 ml (½ cup) coconut water
1 whole pear, skin on, cored and sliced
juice of ½ lemon
handful of ice

This juice eliminates bloat and promotes lower-intestinal health. It is great for kids and adults, especially after indulgences that cause digestive imbalance.

COLD KILLER

Serves 1

125 ml (½ cup) coconut water
6 fresh blueberries
2 slices cucumber, skin on
3 baby spinach leaves
1 tablespoon chopped flat-leaf (Italian) parsley
½ green apple, skin on, cored and chopped
40 g (¼ cup) fresh pineapple, peeled and sliced
squeeze of lemon juice
squeeze of lime juice

DETOX JUICE

Serves 1

125 ml (½ cup) coconut water
25 g (½ cup) baby spinach leaves, roughly chopped
1 wedge fresh pineapple, peeled and roughly chopped
½ cucumber, skin on, roughly chopped
squeeze of lime juice
handful of ice
handful of fresh mint leaves

Belly Balancer

Detox Juice

Cold Killer

This slice is my ultimate go-to for a snack on the run. On the days when everything seems to go wrong, one thing always goes right: this slice. It's easy to make and is packed with clean, energy-promoting ingredients.

ENERGY SLICE

Picture page 153

Makes 12–16 squares

50 g (½ cup) almond meal

45 g (½ cup) shredded coconut, plus extra for sprinkling

60 g (½ cup) sunflower seeds

60 g (½ cup) rolled oats

60 g (½ cup) sultanas

175 g (½ cup) rice malt syrup or honey, plus extra for drizzling

1 egg white, beaten (optional)

1 tablespoon cacao powder (optional)

Preheat the oven to 180°C (350°F).

Combine all the dry ingredients in a bowl. Add the rice malt syrup and egg white, if using. (I like to include it as it adds some extra protein.) Mix until well combined.

Line a 20 x 20 cm (8 x 8 in) brownie tin with baking paper. Add the mixture and press down until it is compacted and smooth. Drizzle with a little extra rice malt syrup and sprinkle over some additional shredded coconut. I also love to top mine with cacao powder for a chocolatey kick.

Bake in the oven for 15 minutes, then remove and leave to cool completely before slicing. Store in an airtight container for up to 2 weeks.

Tip *Serve with a handful of fresh blueberries for a complete and nutritious snack.*

SPICED VANILLA BANANA SMOOTHIE

Serves 1

2 peeled, frozen bananas
1 scoop vanilla protein powder
1 tablespoon ground cinnamon
125 ml (½ cup) almond milk or milk of your choice
125 ml (½ cup) coconut water

Combine all the ingredients in a blender and blitz until smooth. Pour into a chilled jar or glass.

Picture page 153

MUESLI

Makes approx. 640 g

125 g (1 cup) rolled oats
125 g (1 cup) slivered almonds
90 g (1 cup) shredded coconut
60 g (½ cup) sunflower seeds
70 g (½ cup) pepitas (pumpkin seeds)
175 g (½ cup) rice malt syrup

Preheat the oven to 180°C (350°F). Line a 20 x 20 cm (8 x 8 in) brownie tin with baking paper.

Scatter all the dry ingredients in the tin and mix to combine. Drizzle over the rice malt syrup and bake for 10 minutes. Remove from the oven and stir the mixture, then continue baking for another 10–15 minutes until evenly golden brown.

Remove from the oven and leave to cool, then store in an airtight container for up to 1 week.

Tip Try adding hazelnuts, walnuts, uncooked quinoa, sesame seeds or peanuts to your muesli.

Fit Mama fuel

LUNCH

Lunches in the Fit Mama program are designed to be easily transportable and nourishing to keep you feeling full and satisfied during a busy day. Many of the recipes can be prepared using leftovers from dinner the night before, or can be quickly prepared in the morning.

Lunch is an important meal and should be something substantial with plenty of complex carbohydrates. Eating a good lunch will help you avoid that 3 pm energy dip and stop you grazing too much before dinner. This is the time to pad your meal with extra salad, extra fruit and definitely extra protein. Top your salad with tuna and eggs, or add a bit of cooked rice or pasta.

Picnic Pie
(recipe page 160)

Warm Italian Salad
(recipe page 161)

This delicious baked breakfast or lunch pie is so easy to prepare and pack up. It's perfect for lunchboxes, too.

PICNIC PIE

Picture page 159

Serves 4-6

Base

100 g (1 cup) LSA (linseed, sunflower seed and almond) mix
185 g (1 cup) pre-cooked rice mixed with chia seeds
30 g (¼ cup) sunflower seeds
1 egg
2 tablespoons rice bran oil
salt and pepper

Filling

4 eggs
2 tablespoons milk
200 g (7 oz) feta cheese
handful of cherry tomatoes, chopped
1 spring onion (scallion), sliced
handful of baby spinach, sliced

Preheat the oven to 200°C (400°F). Grease and line a 20 x 20 cm (8 x 8 in) pie or flan tin.

For the base, mix together all of the ingredients, then press into the bottom of the prepared tin.

To make the filling, combine all of the ingredients in a bowl, then pour over the base. Transfer to the oven and bake for 20 minutes, or until the eggs are completely cooked. Leave to cool completely before cutting.

Serve warm with a salad, or slice up into easy-to-manage pieces for kids.

WARM ITALIAN SALAD

Picture page 159

Serves 4

3 zucchini (courgettes), grated
2 tablespoons garlic oil
salt and pepper
200 g (7 oz) whole button mushrooms
200 g (7 oz) tomatoes, diced
200 g (7 oz) feta cheese, crumbled
1 bunch flat-leaf (Italian) parsley, chopped
juice of 1 lemon

Preheat the oven to 180°C (350°F).

Put the zucchini on a baking tray and drizzle with 1 tablespoon garlic oil. Season well with salt and pepper and roast in the oven for about 30 minutes, or until browned and softened. Set aside to cool.

Heat the remaining garlic oil in a frying pan over a medium heat and sauté the mushrooms for 3–5 minutes, or until browned. Set aside.

Combine the tomatoes, feta, parsley and lemon juice in a bowl and season with salt and pepper to taste.

Build the salad by layering the zucchini, mushrooms and tomato mixture on a serving plate.

This salad is perfect for anyone wanting to feel light, lean and healthy. I eat it before I have to attend an event or photo shoot.

CLEAN GREEN TURKEY SALAD

Serves 4

1 tablespoon olive oil
500 g (1 lb 2 oz) turkey mince
salt and pepper
1 corn cob, boiled, steamed or chargrilled
95 g (½ cup) pre-cooked brown rice (or 150 g/½ cup chia seeds)
1 green apple, skin on, cored and diced
25 g (½ cup) baby spinach leaves
1 spring onion (scallion), sliced
2 parsley sprigs, finely chopped
juice of 1 lime
½ avocado, sliced
Lime wedges, to serve

Heat the olive oil in a frying pan over a medium heat and fry the turkey mince until brown. Season with a little salt and pepper. Set aside to cool slightly.

Cut the chargrilled kernals off the corn cob and add to a large bowl. Add all the remaining ingredients and mix lightly to combine. Add the cooled turkey mince and toss gently. Garnish with lime wedges and serve immediately.

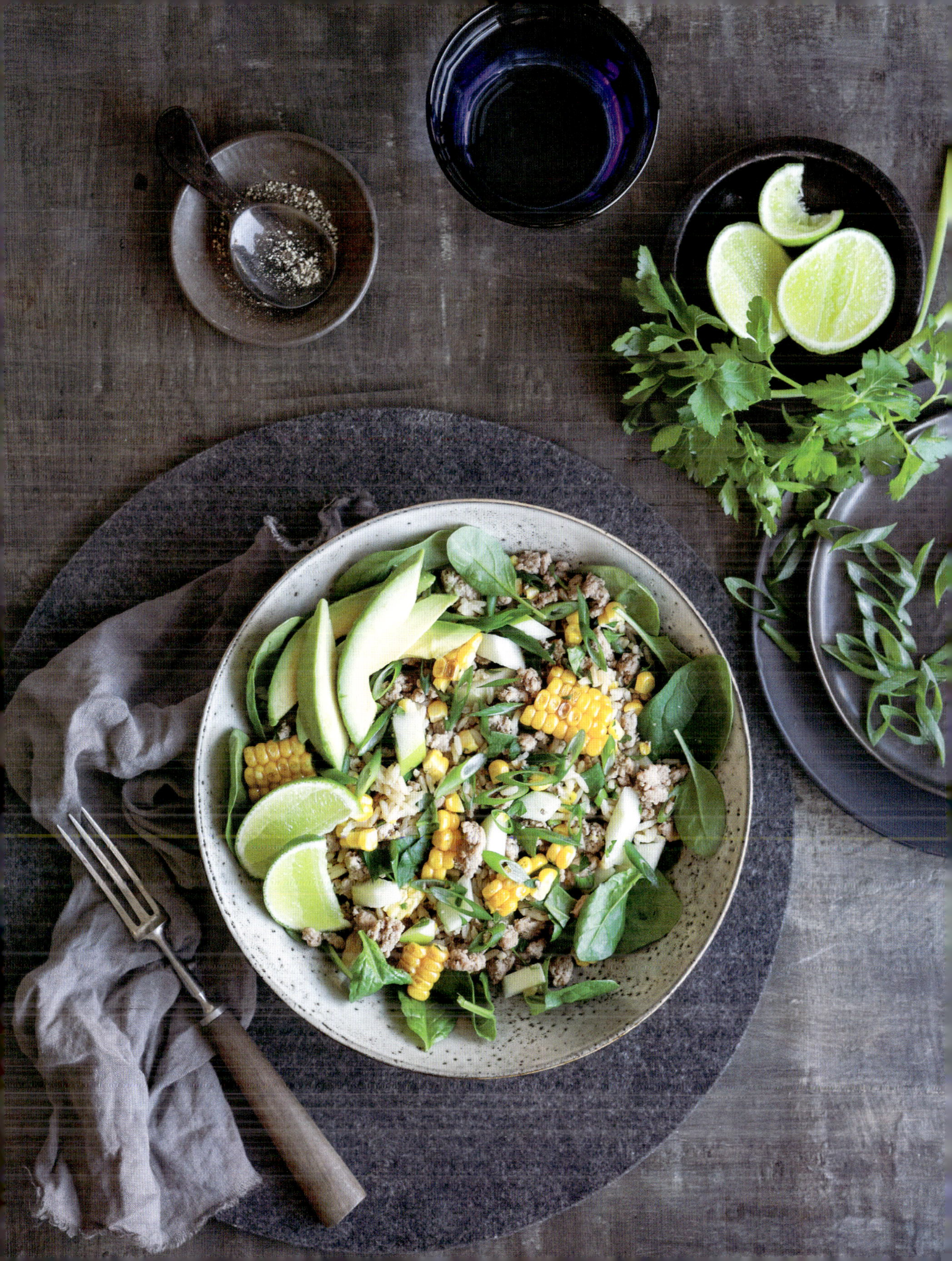

GREEN GRAINY SLICE

Makes 12 squares

Base
100 g (1 cup) LSA (linseed, sunflower seed and almond) mix
100 g (1 cup) almond meal
60 g (½ cup) sunflower seeds
salt and pepper
2 eggs, lightly beaten
3 tablespoons rice bran oil

Filling
8 eggs
1 bunch baby spinach, roughly chopped
200 g (7 oz) feta cheese, crumbled
1 bunch (approx. 8 spears) fresh asparagus
2 tablespoons pine nuts

Preheat the oven to 180°C (350°F). Line a 20 x 20 cm (8 x 8 in) brownie tin with baking paper.

For the base, combine all the dry ingredients in a bowl, then add the eggs and oil and mix together well. Press the mixture firmly into the base of the prepared tray. Transfer to the oven and bake for 15 minutes, then remove but leave the oven on.

To make the filling, beat the eggs in a large bowl, then mix in the spinach and feta. Pour the mixture over the warm base.

Lay the asparagus spears on top of the egg mixture, then sprinkle over the pine nuts. Bake for an additional 20 minutes, or until the egg is fully cooked and the asparagus and nuts are golden. Cut while warm.

Satisfy those cheese cravings

MISO SOUP

Serves 4

3 tablespoons garlic rice bran oil
250 g (9 oz) chicken thighs, diced
1 bunch spring onions (scallions), thinly sliced, plus extra to garnish
1 bunch bok choy (pak choy), thinly sliced
10 closed cup mushrooms, sliced
2 tablespoons vegetable stock
2 tablespoons chicken stock
200 g (7 oz) rice noodles
1 tablespoon rice bran oil
250 g (9 oz) herbed halloumi cheese, sliced
4 large handfuls baby spinach leaves, to serve
1 tablespoon sesame seeds

Heat the garlic oil in a large stockpot over a medium heat and fry the chicken thighs until browned.

Add the spring onions, bok choy and mushrooms, reduce the heat to low and cook gently until just wilted to allow the flavours to infuse.

Add 750 ml (3 cups) water, or enough to submerge the chicken and vegetables. Add the vegetable and chicken stock, followed by the noodles, then cover with a lid and simmer gently for 10 minutes.

While the soup simmers, heat the rice bran oil in a frying pan over a medium heat and fry the halloumi slices on both sides until golden brown. Set aside.

When the noodles have floated to the top of the soup, it is ready. Serve with spinach leaves, halloumi, sesame seeds and some extra fresh spring onions.

SNACKS

Getting your snacking right is a key part to eating a balanced diet. Snacks keep the metabolism firing throughout the day, and they offer little bursts of helpful protein and carbohydrates to keep our energy levels high.

There is nothing wrong with factoring snacks into your day—in fact, it helps to prevent hunger, which leads to overeating. However, be careful that your snacks don't turn into a meal. Portion out your snacks for the day, and store them in individual bags or containers. Combine a glass of water or two with your snack to help increase the feeling of fullness.

Sweet Crispy Bread Topped with Yoghurt and Fruit
(recipe page 168)

Iced Chocolate Smoothie
(recipe page 170)

Apricot Cashew Protein Balls
(recipe page 169)

SWEET CRISPY BREAD TOPPED with YOGHURT and FRUIT

Picture page 167

Serves 6

50 g (½ cup) almond meal
60 g (½ cup) sunflower seeds
70 g (½ cup) pepitas (pumpkin seeds)
75 g (½ cup) currants
75 g (½ cup) coconut flour
150 g (½ cup) chia seeds
105 g (½ cup) coconut oil
175 g (½ cup) rice malt syrup

1 apple, skin on, sliced, to serve
155 g (1 cup) fresh berries, to serve
150 g (5½ oz) yoghurt, to serve

Preheat the oven to 180°C (350°F). Grease and line a baking tray.

Combine all the bread ingredients in a blender and blitz until well mixed. Press into the base of the prepared tray. Transfer to the oven and bake for 20 minutes, or until crispy.

Remove from the oven and leave to cool completely. Cut or snap the bread into pieces and top with the apple, berries and yoghurt.

CHOCOLATE PROTEIN BALLS

Makes 12

155 g (1 cup) raw cashews, walnuts or almonds
55 g (½ cup) almond meal
1 scoop chocolate protein powder (or your favourite protein)
60 g (½ cup) cacao powder
1 tablespoon coconut oil
45 g (½ cup) shredded coconut, plus extra for rolling (optional)

Put the nuts, almond meal, protein powder and cacao powder in a blender and blitz until the nuts release their oil. Add the coconut oil and shredded coconut and blitz again until evenly combined.

Roll the mixture into bite-size balls and store in an airtight container in the refrigerator for up to 5 days. If desired, roll the balls again in the extra coconut before storing.

Picture page 151

APRICOT CASHEW PROTEIN BALLS

Makes 12

155 g (1 cup) raw cashews
180 g (1 cup) dried apricots
50 g (½ cup) almond meal
1 scoop vanilla protein powder
1 tablespoon coconut oil
45 g (½ cup) shredded coconut, plus extra for rolling (optional)

Combine the cashews, apricots, almond meal and protein powder in a blender. Blitz until the cashews release their oil. Add the coconut oil and shredded coconut and blitz again until evenly combined.

Roll the mixture into bite-size balls and store in an airtight container in the refrigerator for up to 5 days. If desired, roll the balls again in the extra coconut before storing.

Picture pages 151 & 167

FAVE SMOOTHIE

Serves 1

250 ml (1 cup) almond milk or milk your choice
60 ml (¼ cup) coconut water
1 peeled, frozen banana
1 scoop chocolate protein powder
1 tablespoon almond butter or your choice of nut or seed butter, plus extra to garnish
1 teaspoon cacao nibs, plus extra to garnish

Combine all the ingredients in a blender and blitz until smooth and creamy.

Pour into a serving glass or jar and garnish with extra almond butter and cacao nibs.

Picture page 173

CARAMEL SMOOTHIE

Serves 1

250 ml (1 cup) almond milk or milk of your choice
1 scoop vanilla protein powder (optional)
½ fresh banana, peeled
handful of ice
1 tablespoon good-quality caramel sauce

Combine the milk, protein powder, banana and ice in a blender and blitz until smooth.

Drizzle the caramel sauce around the inside of a clean serving glass or jar. Pour in the smoothie and serve.

ICED CHOCOLATE SMOOTHIE

Serves 1

185 ml (¾ cup) almond milk or milk of your choice
1 peeled, frozen banana
2½ tablespoons coconut yoghurt
1 tablespoon cacao powder
1 scoop chocolate protein powder

Combine the milk, banana, ½ tablespoon yoghurt, the cacao powder and protein powder in a blender and blitz until thick and smooth.

Drizzle the remaining 2 tablespoons yoghurt around the inside of a clean glass or jar. Pour in the smoothie and serve.

Picture page 167

BANANA BREAD

Makes 1 loaf

5 ripe bananas, peeled and mashed
1 egg
180 g (1¾ cups) almond meal
2 tablespoons ground cinnamon
2 tablespoons coconut oil

Topping
2 tablespoons slivered almonds
10 pecans (or other nuts)
2 tablespoons sesame seeds
2 tablespoons shredded coconut

3 tablespoons rice malt syrup, for drizzling
natural yoghurt, to serve

Preheat the oven to 180°C (350°F). Grease and line a 17 x 26 cm (6½ x 10½ in) loaf (bar) tin.

Combine the banana and egg in a bowl and mash with a fork. Add the almond meal, cinnamon and coconut oil and mix well. Pour the mixture into the prepared tin. Top with the almonds, pecans, sesame seeds and coconut, then bake in the oven for 30 minutes, or until the top is golden brown.

Remove from the oven and leave to cool for 15 minutes. Drizzle with rice malt syrup and serve with thick natural yoghurt on the side.

This slice is raw, vegan, and it tastes like a Snickers bar.

ENVY SLICE

Makes 9 squares

Base
235 g (1½ cups) cashews
2 tablespoons cacao powder, plus extra to garnish
2 tablespoons coconut oil
8 dates, pitted

Filling
2 peeled, frozen bananas
4 tablespoons peanut butter
40 g (¼ cup) whole almonds

Grease and line a 20 x 20 cm (8 x 8 in) brownie or slice tin.

To make the base, combine the cashews, cacao powder, coconut oil and dates in a blender and blitz to a rough crumb.

Press the mixture into the bottom of the prepared tray and refrigerate while you make the filling.

Wash the blender, then add the filling ingredients and blend until smooth. Spread the filling evenly on top of the base, then sprinkle over some extra cacao powder to finish.

Refrigerate again for about 30 minutes to firm up. The top will remain quite soft, so store any leftovers in the refrigerator.

Fave Smoothie
(recipe page 170)

Envy Slice

WHOLEGRAIN BREAD

The bread is ideal for when you're craving carbohydrates and need a quick snack. It's great topped with nut butter, hummus, avocado, yoghurt and fruit—anything you like. It's perfect for lunchboxes or serving on the side of bigger meals.

Makes 1 loaf

200 g (2 cups) almond meal
50 g (½ cup) LSA (linseed, sunflower seed and almond) mix
70 g (½ cup) pepitas (pumpkin seeds)
150 g (½ cup) chia seeds
80 g (½ cup) pine nuts
½ tablespoon salt
2 eggs, beaten
3 tablespoons garlic-infused olive oil
2 tablespoons coconut oil

Preheat the oven to 180°C (350°F). Grease a baking tray and line with baking paper.

Combine all the dry ingredients in a large bowl. Pour in the beaten eggs, then add the oils. Mix until evenly combined.

Press the mixture into the bottom of the baking tray to a 2 cm (¾ in) thickness. Transfer to the oven and bake for about 25 minutes, or until golden brown.

Remove from the oven and cut slits in the top of the bread. This will help it to crisp up as it cools. Leave to cool completely before slicing.

Serve with soups, as crackers with dips, or with any of your favourite toppings. Store the bread in an airtight container for up to 5 days. (If it's summer, store it in the fridge.)

HEAVENLY HUMMUS

Makes 330 g (1½ cups)

1 x 400 g (14 oz) tin chickpeas, drained
1 garlic clove
1 tablespoon sweet chilli sauce
handful of fresh basil leaves
salt and pepper
cooked rice pasta, wholegrain bread or rice cakes, to serve

Combine all the ingredients in a food processor or blender and blitz to a smooth paste.

Serve stirred through cooked rice pasta, or on top of wholegrain bread or rice cakes.

BEETROOT DIP

Makes 330 g (1½ cups)

1 x 425 g (15 oz) tin whole baby beetroot, drained
155 g (1 cup) whole raw cashews
1 tablespoon tahini
1 tablespoon garlic-infused olive oil
squeeze of lemon juice

Combine all the ingredients in a blender and blitz until smooth.

Serve as a dip, or use on salad, toast, nachos or tacos—the list really is endless.

Fit Mama fuel 175

DINNER

Dinner is the time when our family gets together to talk about the highs and lows of the day. Finding this time can be difficult, but everyone benefits from it.

Dinner should be quick to prepare and easy to digest, assisting with sleep and recovery. I avoid anything too dense at this time of day so I can go to bed feeling light and satisfied.

I find that sticking to the same menu plan for a two-week period helps us to get organised. The only trick is getting enough variation in there to avoid boredom. I let the kids give me ideas for what they'd like and then look at how I can work them into the fortnightly plan. We tend to vary our dinners from things like meatballs with zoodles (zucchini noodles) to tacos with turkey mince, salad and tortillas, and teriyaki salmon with greens and quinoa.

Zucchini Quiche
(recipe page 179)

Chicken Teriyaki
(recipe page 178)

CHICKEN TERIYAKI

Picture page 177

Serves 4

- 3 tablespoons rice bran oil
- 500 g (1 lb 2 oz) chicken thighs, cut into strips
- salt and pepper
- 370 g (2 cups) cooked brown rice and quinoa mix
- 130 g (1 cup) frozen peas, cooked
- 3 shallots, finely chopped
- 1 iceberg lettuce, finely shredded
- 100 ml (3½ fl oz) shop-bought chicken teriyaki sauce (see Tip)
- 1 avocado, sliced
- 4 tablespoons coconut yoghurt

Heat the oil in a frying pan over a medium heat and fry the chicken until brown. Season with salt and pepper. Transfer the chicken to a plate lined with paper towel to cool and drain.

Reheat the rice and quinoa mix in the microwave for 2 minutes, or until hot, then transfer to a bowl. Mix in the cooked peas and chopped shallots, then transfer the mixture to a serving plate.

Top the rice with the lettuce and place the chicken on top. Pour over the teriyaki sauce and serve with the sliced avocado and coconut yoghurt.

Tip The best quality teriyaki sauces can be found at your local Asian grocer.

If you are short on time and cannot really be bothered to cook but want a nutritious, unbelievably delicious dinner, then this is the one. It's a clean-eating meal that has a crispy, nutty garlic base with a quiche-style topping. It is great for lunches and is a delicious favourite among the family.

ZUCCHINI QUICHE

Picture page 177

Serves 6

Base
50 g (½ cup) LSA (linseed, sunflower seed and almond) mix
70 g (½ cup) pepitas (pumpkin seeds)
60 g (½ cup) sunflower seeds
pinch of salt
2 tablespoons garlic rice bran oil
1 egg, beaten

Topping
6 eggs
½ red onion, diced
100 g (3½ oz) feta cheese (as required), crumbled
2 sprigs flat-leaf (Italian) parsley, roughly chopped
2 zucchini (courgettes), sliced into 8 cm (3¼ in) lengths and roasted
salt and pepper

Preheat the oven to 200°C (400°F). Grease and line a 25 cm (10 in) flan dish.

To make the base, combine the dry ingredients in a bowl, then add the oil and egg. Mix until evenly combined, then press the mixture over the base of the prepared dish.

Transfer to the oven and bake for 10 minutes (you can roast your zucchini at the same time), then remove but leave the oven on.

For the topping, beat the eggs in another bowl, then pour on top of the base. Scatter over the onion, feta and parsley, then arrange the zucchini slices on top. Season with salt and pepper. Return to the oven and bake for another 15 minutes.

Serve with salad or on its own, hot or cold.

Fit Mama fuel

Serve these burgers with a simple salad or in a bread roll with your favourite toppings.

VEGIE BURGERS

Serves 6-8

4 wholegrain tortillas

Burgers
1 x 425 g (15 oz) tin brown lentils, drained
3 zucchini (courgettes), grated
2 tablespoons sweet chilli sauce
1 egg
340 g (1½ cups) leftover mashed vegetables (page 185)
110 g (¾ cup) coconut flour
salt and pepper
3 tablespoons rice bran oil

Salad
large handful of spinach leaves
¼ red cabbage, shredded
1 carrot, grated
1 tablespoon soy sauce
1 tablespoon lemon juice
pinch of coconut sugar

Combine all the burger ingredients, except the oil, in a bowl and mix well. Season to taste with salt and pepper.

Roll the mixture into palm-size balls and set aside. You should get 6–8 burgers out of the mixture.

Heat the oil in a large frying pan over a medium heat and fry the tortillas, one at a time, until golden and crisp. Set aside. Add a little more oil if necessary and fry the vegie burgers, flipping once, until golden brown on both sides. Set aside to cool a little.

For the salad, combine the spinach leaves, cabbage and carrot in a serving bowl. In another small bowl, mix together the soy sauce, lemon juice and sugar and use it to dress the salad. Toss well to combine.

Serve the vegie burgers with the salad and crispy tortillas.

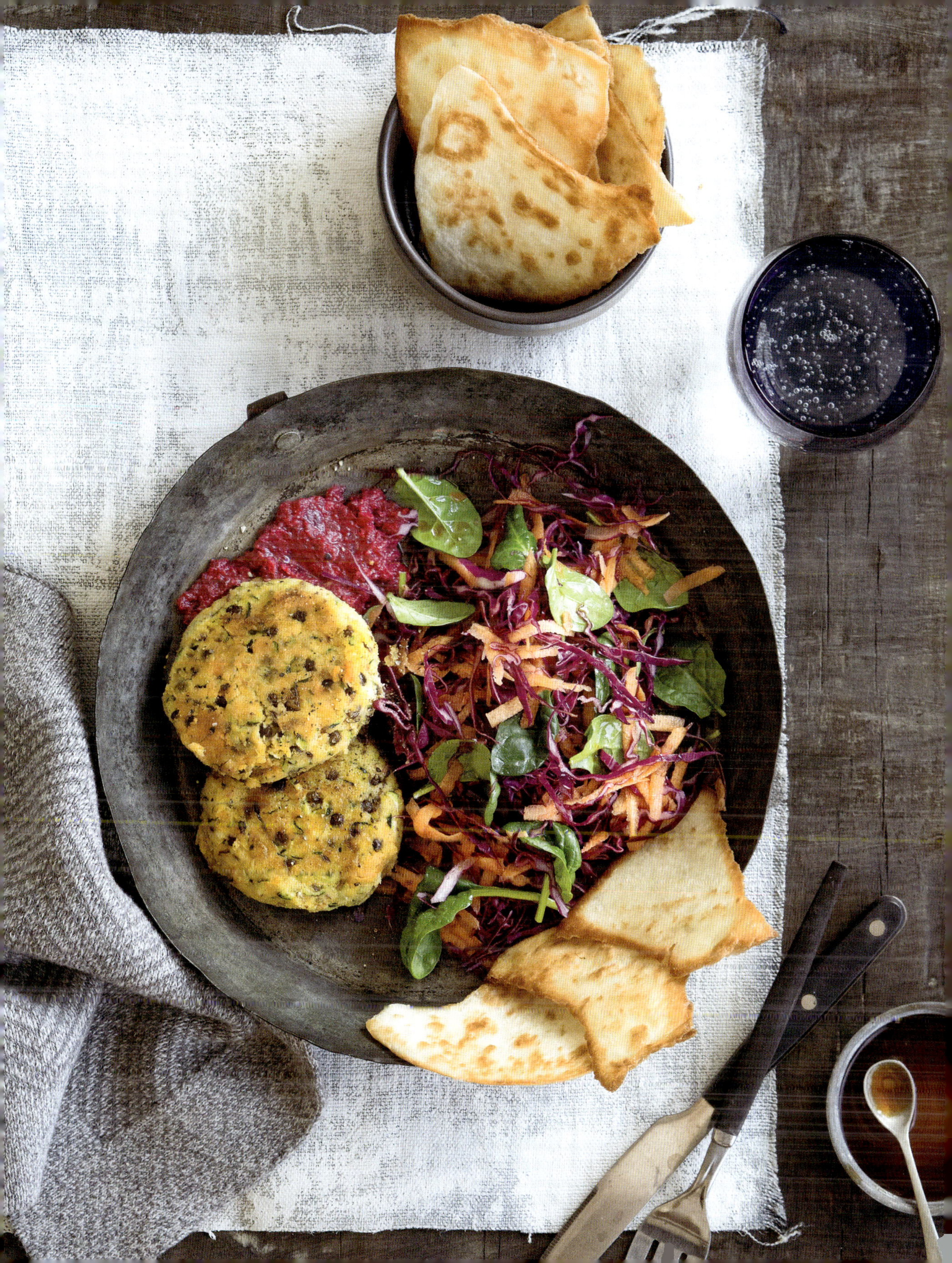

BAKED EGG PIE *with* HALLOUMI

Serves 4

8 eggs
28 cherry tomatoes, sliced
150 g (5½ oz) halloumi cheese,
　cut into cubes
2 handfuls of baby spinach leaves
salt and pepper
4 tablespoons chopped spring onion
　(scallion)
4 tablespoons onion relish, to serve

Preheat the oven to 180°C (350°F).

Crack the eggs into an ovenproof baking dish. Scatter the sliced tomatoes and halloumi over the eggs and the spinach around the edge.

Transfer to the oven and bake for 20–25 minutes, then place under a hot grill for 2 minutes to brown the top.

Season with salt and pepper to taste and scatter over the spring onion. Serve with onion relish on the side.

When I host brunch at my place, I usually make this pie. It's absolutely delicious and free of any nasties.

SWEET POTATO PIE

Serves 4

Base
100 g (1 cup) LSA (linseed, sunflower seed and almond) mix
185 g (1 cup) pre-cooked brown rice (or use 300 g/1 cup chia seeds)
30 g (¼ cup) sunflower seeds
1 egg, beaten
2 tablespoons rice bran oil
salt and pepper

Filling
5 eggs, beaten
150 g (5½ oz) feta cheese (or as much as you like), crumbled
1 spring onion (scallion), sliced
handful of baby spinach, sliced
1 large sweet potato, peeled, cut into 2 cm (¾ in) lengths and roasted
salt and pepper

Preheat the oven to 200°C (400°F). Grease and line a 28 x 14 cm (11¼ x 5½ in) pie or flan dish.

To make the base, mix all of the ingredients together in a bowl, then press the mixture into the base of the prepared dish. Transfer to the oven and bake for 10 minutes.

Meanwhile, prepare the filling. Combine all of the ingredients except the sweet potato in a bowl and toss.

Remove the base from the oven and pour in the filling. Arrange the sweet potato wedges in a wheel shape on top of the egg mixture, then return to the oven and cook for 20 minutes, or until the egg is thoroughly cooked. Remove and set aside to cool a little and set before cutting.

Serve warm alongside a salad or slice up for kids to enjoy as a snack.

Such a delicious, healthy and filling dinner!

GREEK CHICKEN with QUINOA and SALAD

Serves 4

Greek spice mix (see Note)
2 chicken breasts or 4 chicken thighs
salt and pepper
2 tablespoons rice bran oil
150 g (5½ oz) halloumi cheese
handful of mixed salad leaves
370 g (2 cups) cooked brown rice and quinoa mix

Rub the spice mix into the chicken with some salt and pepper, then set aside.

Heat 1 tablespoon of the oil in a frying pan over a medium heat and pan-fry the chicken until completely cooked. Remove and set aside.

Add the remaining oil and fry the halloumi until golden brown on both sides.

When you're ready to serve, slice the chicken and halloumi. Scatter the salad over a serving plate, add the cooked rice and quinoa, then top with the chicken and halloumi.

Note You can make your own Greek spice mix by combining crushed garlic, fresh oregano, basil and dill, and grated lemon zest.

This vegetable mash is versatile and can be served with a variety of different proteins, but it also makes a great stand-alone dish when you're looking for something simple.

PESTO PASTA

Serves 4

large handful of fresh basil leaves
2 tablespoons rice bran oil
80 g (½ cup) pine nuts
salt and pepper
250 g (9 oz) spaghetti
200 g (7 oz) fresh cherry tomatoes, quartered
100 g (3½ oz) feta cheese, crumbled

Combine the basil leaves, oil, pine nuts and a generous amount of salt and pepper in a food processor. Blitz to a coarse paste.

Bring a saucepan of salted water to the boil and cook the spaghetti according to the packet instructions. Drain and transfer to a large serving bowl.

Add the pesto to the spaghetti and gently toss to coat. Carefully mix through the tomatoes and the feta. Season with freshly cracked salt and pepper and serve.

MASHED VEGETABLES

Serves 4

1 large sweet potato
1 head broccoli
½ Kent pumpkin (squash)

Peel the sweet potato and cut into small cubes. Cut the broccoli head into small florets.

Cut the skin off the pumpkin and scoop out the seeds, then discard. Cut the flesh into small cubes, about the same size as the sweet potato.

Put the vegetables in the top half of a double-boiler and cover with the lid. Fill the bottom half with water and set over a medium–low heat. Bring to a gentle simmer and steam until the vegetables are just cooked.

Transfer the vegetables to a bowl and mash together well. Store in airtight containers in the fridge or freezer to be used throughout the week.

DESSERTS

I believe in balance and keeping your sanity, and that means having a dessert every now and then. Fit Mama desserts are designed to crush any sugar cravings, and most are healthier versions of dishes you probably already love. They contain wholesome, nourishing ingredients with the added kick of a bit of extra sweetness, so you can enjoy them without the guilt. These never last long in our house, and we like to share them at the kitchen bench, all digging in with spoons.

Coconut Parfait with Tropical Coconut Crunch
(recipe page 189)

Coconut Iceblocks
(recipe page 188)

COCONUT ICEBLOCKS

Picture page 187

Makes 6

185 g (¾ cup) coconut yoghurt
1 scoop vanilla protein powder (optional)
155 g (1 cup) fresh berries, plus extra to serve
125 ml (½ cup) melted chocolate (about 100 g/3½ oz solid chocolate), to serve

You will also need
6 ice-cream moulds
6 wooden popsicle sticks (see Tip)

Mix together the yoghurt, protein powder (if using) and berries in a bowl. Divide the mixture between the ice-cream moulds and insert a wooden popsicle stick about half way into the mixture.

Freeze for about 4 hours before serving with fresh berries or melted chocolate swirls.

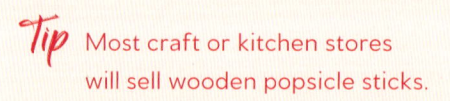

Tip Most craft or kitchen stores will sell wooden popsicle sticks.

Dive into summer with fresh mango, banana and toasted coconut. This clean, delicious breakfast, dessert or snack is also dairy-free. Enjoy!

COCONUT PARFAIT with TROPICAL COCONUT CRUNCH

Picture page 187

Serves 2

1 mango, peeled and pitted, diced
1 banana, peeled and sliced
1 tablespoon coconut yoghurt
100 g (½ cup) Coconut Crunch (see right)
1 tablespoon shredded coconut, to serve (optional)

Layer all the ingredients in half of a cut fresh coconut or a serving bowl.

For extra coconutty goodness, finish with a sprinkle of shredded coconut.

Coconut Crunch

45 g (½ cup) shredded coconut
125 g (1 cup) rolled oats
45 g (½ cup) dessicated coconut
1 tablespoon rice malt syrup
75 g (¼ cup) banana chips
70 g (½ cup) pepitas (pumpkin seeds)

Preheat the oven to 180°C (350°F). Line a 20 x 20 cm (8 x 8 in) brownie tin (or any similar tray) with baking paper.

Combine all the ingredients in a bowl, then scatter over the prepared tray and toast in the oven for 20 minutes, turning halfway through.

Leave to cool completely, then store in an airtight container for up to 1 week.

I love warm hot cross buns with melting butter, but unfortunately they do not like me. To satisfy my cravings, I make this Hot Cross Bun Jar instead. It is a clean-eating dessert or snack for any time of the day, and it really hits the spot.

HOT CROSS BUN JAR

Serves 1

Base
2 tablespoons almond meal
1 teaspoon ground cinnamon
1 tablespoon shredded coconut
1 tablespoon rice malt syrup

1 peeled, frozen banana
½ teaspoon ground cinnamon, plus extra to garnish
¼ green apple, skin on, grated
1 tablespoon coconut yoghurt
1 teaspoon currants, plus extra to garnish

For the base, combine all the ingredients in a bowl, then spoon the mixture into the bottom of a clean serving glass or jar.

Combine the banana, cinnamon, apple and yoghurt in a blender and blitz until smooth. Add the currants and stir in gently.

Scoop the banana mixture into the jar and finish with some extra currants and cinnamon for spice.

APPLE PIE JAR

Serves 1

60 g (½ cup) Muesli (page 157)
1 green apple, skin on, grated
125 g (½ cup) coconut yoghurt
1 teaspoon ground cinnamon

Put the muesli in the bottom of a clean serving glass or jar. Top with the grated apple, then the coconut yoghurt, and finish with a sprinkle of cinnamon.

LEMON MERINGUE PIE JAR

Serves 1

60 g (½ cup) Muesli (page 157)
1 peeled, frozen banana
2 heaped tablespoons coconut yoghurt
zest and juice of 1 lemon, plus 1 lemon wheel to garnish
juice of 1 lime
1 teaspoon coconut sugar

Add the muesli to a clean serving glass or jar.

Blend the banana, 1 tablespoon coconut yoghurt and the citrus juices and zest until smooth and creamy. Pour into the serving glass on top of the muesli.

Add the remaining coconut yoghurt and top with the coconut sugar and the lemon wheel.

BLACKBERRY, CHOCOLATE and CACAO NIB JAR

Serves 1

1 tablespoon cacao nibs, plus extra to serve
80 g (½ cup) fresh blueberries
125 g (½ cup) chocolate-flavoured coconut yoghurt
30 g (¼ cup) fresh blackberries

Add half the cacao nibs to a clean serving glass or jar and top with the blueberries.

Add most of the chocolate yoghurt, saving a little to garnish. Add the remaining cacao nibs, then the blackberries. Finish with the remaining yoghurt and top with some extra cacao nibs.

Tip If you can't find chocolate-flavoured coconut yoghurt, use normal yoghurt and mix in 1 tablespoon cacao powder until well combined.

Picture page 193

Fit Mama fuel

CHOCOLATE CARAMEL CUP

Serves 1

125 ml (½ cup) almond milk or milk of your choice
1 peeled, frozen banana
2 tablespoons cacao powder
2 medjool dates, pitted
2 tablespoons Muesli (page 157)
1 teaspoon good-quality caramel sauce
2 pieces store-bought coconut toffee (optional)

Combine the almond milk, banana, cacao powder and dates in a blender and blitz until smooth. Pour into a small serving glass or jar.

Sprinkle the muesli on one side of the glass or jar, then carefully pour in the caramel sauce on the other side. Finish with the coconut toffee, if using.

CHOCOLATE CHIA CUP

Serves 1

3 tablespoons chia seeds
1 tablespoon cacao powder
60 ml (¼ cup) coconut water (or chocolate-flavoured coconut water)
1 tablespoon coconut or Greek yoghurt
80 g (½ cup) blueberries
handful of chocolate-coated blueberries, chocolate chips or carob-coated ginger
rice malt syrup or honey, for drizzling

Combine the chia seeds with the cacao powder, coconut water and yoghurt in a bowl. Mix well, then refrigerate for 30 minutes.

Scoop the chia mixture into a serving glass or jar and top with the blueberries, chocolate-coated blueberries and a drizzle of rice malt syrup.

Blackberry, Chocolate, and Cacao Nib Jar
(recipe page 191)

Clean, Mean Chocolate Cake
(recipe page 195)

Chocolate Caramel Cup

When you're craving something indulgent

GOO GOO PIE

Serves 1

1 banana, peeled and sliced
60 g (¼ cup) plain coconut yoghurt
60 g (¼ cup) chocolate-flavoured coconut yoghurt (see Tip page 191)
2 tablespoons slivered almonds
1 tablespoon good-quality caramel sauce
1 tablespoon cacao powder, to garnish

Start by layering half the sliced banana into a serving glass or jar, followed by half the plain coconut yoghurt.

Next, add half the chocolate-flavoured yoghurt, followed by a little more banana. Sprinkle over most of the almonds, reserving a few to garnish.

Add half the caramel sauce, then the remaining plain coconut yoghurt. Top with the remaining caramel sauce and chocolate-flavoured yoghurt.

Sprinkle with cacao powder and the remaining slivered almonds and banana to garnish.

CLEAN, MEAN CHOCOLATE CAKE

Picture page 193

Serves 8

- 100 g (½ cup) coconut oil
- 375 g (13 oz) good-quality dark chocolate, chopped
- 75 g (½ cup) coconut sugar
- 2 tablespoons almond milk or milk of your choice
- 225 g (2¼ cup) almond meal
- 5 eggs
- 1 tablespoon cacao powder, for dusting
- 3 strawberries, sliced, to decorate

Preheat the oven to 160°C (315°F). Grease and line a 20 cm (8 in) round cake tin.

Combine the coconut oil and chocolate in a heatproof bowl set over a saucepan of simmering water. Heat gently, until the chocolate and oil have melted.

Remove from the heat and mix in the coconut sugar, almond milk and almond meal until thoroughly combined. Add the eggs, one at a time, beating with an electric mixer between each addition.

Pour the mixture into the prepared tin, cover with aluminium foil and bake for 50–60 minutes, or until a skewer inserted in the middle of the cake comes out clean.

Remove the foil and leave the cake to cool before turning out onto a wire rack. Dust with cacao powder and top with sliced strawberries.

Fit Mama fuel

RAW STRAWBERRY 'CHEESECAKE'

Serves 6

Base
6 dried figs
125 g (1 cup) walnuts
45 g (½ cup) flaked almonds
1 heaped tablespoon coconut oil

Filling
310 g (2 cups) unsalted cashews soaked in 375 ml (1½ cups) coconut water overnight
60 g (1 cup) dried strawberries
40 g (½ cup) dried raspberries
220 g (1 cup) frozen strawberries
1 tablespoon rice malt syrup
fresh strawberries and blueberries, to serve
mint leaves, to serve

Grease and line a 20 x 20 cm (8 x 8 in) brownie or slice tray.

To make the base, combine all the ingredients in a blender and blitz to a fine crumb. Press the mixture into the bottom of the prepared tray and refrigerate while you make the filling.

Put the cashews and their soaking water in a food processor and blend until smooth and creamy. Add the remaining ingredients and blend until smooth.

Pour the filling over the base and gently smooth it out. Transfer to the freezer for 1 hour to set.

Serve with fresh strawberries, blueberries and mint leaves.

Tip The longer your cashews soak, the softer and smoother your filling will be.

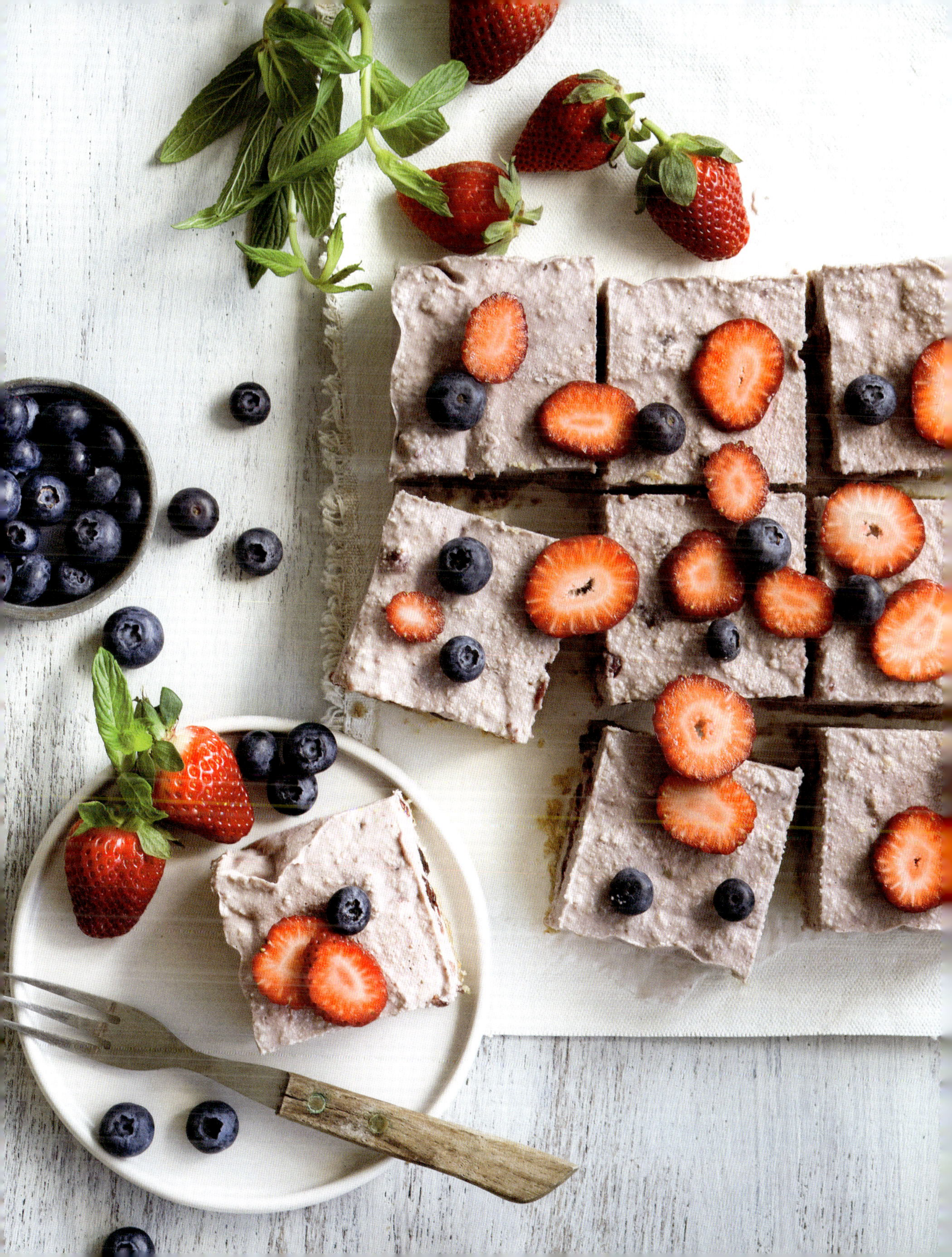

BANANA, CARAMEL *and* PEANUT BUTTER PARFAIT

Serves 1

2 peeled, frozen bananas
1 scoop vanilla protein powder (optional)
2 tablespoons peanut butter or your choice of nut or seed butter
1 fresh banana, peeled and sliced
30 g (¼ cup) rolled oats
125 g (½ cup) coconut yoghurt
1 teaspoon good-quality caramel sauce

Combine the frozen bananas and protein powder, if using, in a blender and blitz to a smooth consistency.

Pour one-third of the blended banana into a clean serving glass or jar. Top with 1 tablespoon of the peanut butter.

Arrange the banana slices around the inside of the glass or jar, then add the oats, reserving a few to garnish.

Dollop in half the yoghurt, then drizzle over half the caramel sauce. Add another third of the blended banana, then the rest of the yoghurt.

Add the remaining blended banana, peanut butter and caramel sauce, and finish with a scattering of oats.

APRICOT CREAM PUFF

Serves 1

80 g (½ cup) frozen mango pieces
3 fresh apricots, pitted (1 diced and 2 halved)
60 ml (¼ cup) almond milk or milk of your choice
1 scoop vanilla protein powder (optional)
1 tablespoon shredded coconut, to garnish

Combine the mango, diced apricot, almond milk and protein powder, if using, in a blender. Blitz to a purée.

Pour the purée into a serving glass or jar, top with the apricot halves and garnish with the coconut.

DAIRY-FREE LAYERED GELATO SUNDAE

Serves 1

3 peeled, frozen bananas
1 scoop vanilla protein powder
1 tablespoon cacao powder
110 g (½ cup) frozen strawberries or raspberries, plus 1 frozen raspberry to serve

Combine the bananas and protein powder in a blender and blitz until smooth, then divide the mixture into three.

Place the first portion of banana mixture into the bottom of a clean serving glass or jar. Next, blend together another portion of the banana mixture with the cacao powder. Add this to the glass in a second layer.

Finally, blend the last portion of banana mixture with the frozen berries until smooth. Add this to the glass on top of the cacao mixture.

Garnish with a frozen raspberry and serve.

DAIRY-FREE BLUEBERRY ICE CREAM

Serves 4

310 g (2 cups) frozen blueberries
60 ml (¼ cup) almond milk or milk of your choice
1 scoop vanilla protein powder (optional)
1 teaspoon coconut yoghurt
fresh blueberries, to garnish

Combine the frozen blueberries, almond milk and protein powder (if using) in a blender and blitz until smooth.

Pour the blueberry mixture into a serving glass or jar, then top with the coconut yoghurt and fresh blueberries.

DAIRY-FREE MANGO GELATO

Serves 4

330 g (2 cups) frozen mango
60 ml (¼ cup) almond milk or milk of your choice
1 scoop vanilla protein powder (optional)
fresh sliced mango, to garnish
1 tablespoon slivered almonds, to garnish

Combine the frozen mango, almond milk and protein powder (if using) in a blender and blitz until smooth.

Pour into a serving glass or jar and top with the fresh mango and almonds.

Picture page 150

This simple, dairy-free ice cream makes a great summer dessert, ideal for Christmas.

DAIRY-FREE RASPBERRY ICE CREAM

Serves 2

2 peeled, frozen bananas
110 g (½ cup) frozen raspberries, plus extra to garnish
1 tablespoon coconut yoghurt

Combine all the ingredients in a blender and blitz until smooth. Scoop into a serving glass or jar and garnish with extra frozen raspberries.

'NUTELLA' LAYERED SUNDAE

Serves 1

Chocolate layer
1 peeled, frozen banana
60 g (¼ cup) coconut yoghurt
1 tablespoon cacao powder
1 teaspoon almond butter or your choice of nut or seed butter

2 tablespoons coconut yoghurt
1 tablespoon almond butter or your choice of nut or seed butter
2 tablespoons chopped almonds and hazelnuts, to garnish

For the chocolate layer, combine all the ingredients in a blender and blitz until smooth.

Pour half of the chocolate layer into the bottom of a serving glass or jar and top with the coconut yoghurt, followed by the almond butter. Finish with the remaining chocolate layer and top with the chopped nuts.

Dairy-free Raspberry Ice Cream

'Nutella' Layered Sundae

Thanks

Thank you to my publisher, Kelly Doust, for your ongoing positivity and confidence, and for your guiding hand. I'll never forget our first phone call. To Andrea O'Connor and Julie Mazur Tribe, for your patience and tireless effort in reading and editing my words. To Madeleine, for making my photos and the truth about my life come alive in book form, and to Carol for holding my hand through the next steps as we look towards the launch and sharing my words with the Fit Mamas of the world.

To my loves and my two very strong and thoughtful children, Zade and Meka, your constant energy and support for the life we share helps me to assist other mums on their journeys. From the very beginning, you have both been conscious, kind young humans, and how blessed I am to call you my son and daughter. I love you, and I am so proud of you both.

To my best friend and confidante, Emma. We have endured so much, and I could not have done this without our banter on bikes, runs, at the pool or our hour-long FaceTime conversations from many places around the world. I love and cherish your friendship immensely.

To my soul sisters and social-media editors, Whitney and Brigette. The idea for this book began with a desire to share some of my favourite recipes and fitness routines with other mums, and these two hardworking, strong women encouraged and supported me every day to create a viable, interesting platform to share my ideas.

A special thank you to Brigette, my creative and artistic eye, for snapping each photo. For your time, your patience and for fixing my straps. You have been instrumental in creating so many of the b. images over the years, as well as many of the photos in this book. How can I ever repay you?

To my mum and my ma, your strength and energy have shown me the truth behind ageing gracefully, living meaningfully and loving fully. My gratitude is endless. I love you both so much.

To the b. crew, without you this book would not have been possible as we are only as good as the people we are surrounded by. You beautiful women keep me positive and motivated every day. Thank you!

To the Hunter, Chris, thanks for picking me up and for always holding me tight.

And to my family and extended family, I love you all.

b.x

Index

A
activewear 90
adrenaline 74
afternoon slump 80, 93, 149
afternoon snacks 149
ageing 71–2, 74
alcohol 64, 77, 85
alignment 55, 56–7
anxiety 21, 33, 64, 74, 101, 102
Apple pie jar 190
apples 147
Apricot cashew protein balls 151, 169
Apricot cream puff 199
athletics 12
autonomy 110

B
bad breath 87
Baked egg pie with halloumi 182
balance, in life 26, 32, 97
balanced diet 88, 92
bananas 147
  Banana bread 171
  Banana, caramel and peanut butter parfait 198
  Dairy-free layered gelato sundae 200
  Envy slice 172
  Goo goo pie 194
  Spiced vanilla banana smoothie 157
barbell hack squat 123
barbell lunge 121
barbell squat 123
beauty, inner 26, 95
beauty regime 91
Beetroot dip 175
Belly balancer 154
bench dip 131
bicep curl with overhead press 125
Blackberry, chocolate and cacao nib jar 191
bloating 80, 82, 86, 87, 91, 93
blueberries 147
  Dairy-free ice cream 201
body 98
  alignment 55, 56–7
  and boredom 50
  caring for 16, 17, 21, 58, 70
  celebrating 72
  cleansing 15
  equilibrium 25, 26
  listening to 63
  optimal function 61
  post-baby 6, 10, 16, 46, 86, 89
  science of 61, 63
  unbalanced 14
body dysmorphia 99
bone strength 16
bones 56
bonus set 116, 141
booty lifter 142
bread
  Banana bread 171
  Sweet crispy bread topped with yoghurt and fruit 168
  Wholegrain bread 151, 174
breakfast 148, 152–7
breastfeeding 15, 21, 71
breathing 64, 66
bulk food buying 147
busyness 40

C
cake, Clean, mean chocolate 195
calm response 105
calories 71
  counting 63, 75, 146
Caramel smoothie 170
carbohydrates (carbs) 76, 79, 85
cardio(vascular) training 15, 48–9, 50, 53, 93
  fasted cardio 48
cashews 196
catastrophising 19
caterpillar plank-row slide 130
caterpillar walkout 126
cellulite 92–3
change management 77, 98, 99–100, 111
'cheesecake', Raw strawberry 196
chewing 77
Chicken teriyaki 178
childbirth 14, 16, 18
children 25, 32, 40, 95, 101–2
  and chores 25, 34, 36–9
  and mum guilt 24, 64
chocolate
  Blackberry, chocolate and cacao nib jar 191
  Chocolate caramel cups 192
  Chocolate chia cups 192
  Chocolate protein balls 151, 169
  Clean mean chocolate cake 195
  Goo goo pie 194
  Iced chocolate smoothie 170
  'Nutella' layered sundae 202
chores, involving children 25, 34, 36–9
Clean green turkey salad 162
Clean mean chocolate cake 195
clothes
  for confidence 89
  selecting 43
Coconut crunch 189
Coconut ice blocks 188
Coconut parfait with tropical coconut crunch 189
coffee 148
Cold killer 154
commitment 99
compassion 95
complaining 109
confirmation bias 98–9
contentment 25
control 102, 104, 109
cooling down 118
core workout 140
cortisol 74
cravings 76–7, 80, 82, 86, 186
crop tops 90
curtsy lunge 120
cycling classes 53

D
Dairy-free blueberry ice cream 201
Dairy-free layered gelato sundae 200
Dairy-free mango gelato 201
Dairy-free raspberry ice cream 202
decision-making 43
deep booty squat 123
delays, in schedule 33
depression, post-natal 20–1, 28, 64
desserts 150, 186–202
determination 99
Detox juice 154
diabetes 81
diary see journalling
dieting 75, 79, 86
digestion 154
dinner 150, 176–85
dip, Beetroot 175
downward-facing dog/energy stretch 132

E
early rising 43, 70–1
eating 11, 63, 70, 72
  eating out 85
  good habits 84, 92
  patterns 77
egg pie, Baked, with halloumi 182
endorphins 77
energy 26, 28, 61, 76, 80, 83, 86, 166
  vampires 109
Energy slice 151, 156
enthusiasm 28–9
Envy slice 172

Index 205

Epsom salts baths 93
equilibrium 25, 26
equipment 118
excuses 100
exercise 6, 12, 15, 53, 63, 70, 74, 146
exercise guide 120–42
exfoliation 91

F
family schedule 34, 35, 41
Fast Fit program 116–17, 139–42
fasted cardio 48
fat loss 152
fatigue 47, 70, 82, 87
fatty deposits 93
Fave smoothie 170
fear 98, 100–2, 105
fight-or-flight response 101
fitness 6–7, 10–11, 13, 61
fitness classes 47
fitness plan 46, 47
fitness training 46–53
  motivation 46–7, 50
  planning 46, 116–18
  and pregnancy 14–15
  regularity 53
  variety 50
fluid retention 58, 59, 60, 93
flutter kicks 131
foam roller chest/spine stretch 133
foam roller stretches 132–3, 142
food 7, 63
  appreciating 75, 87–8
  choices 11
  concept of 76–81
  cravings 76–7, 80, 82, 86, 186
  and fitness 74, 146
  local/seasonal 147
  staples 151
  staying on budget 147
  toxic 86–7
  variety 151, 176
  weight loss promoters 85, 146
freedom 110
freezer use 147, 151
fruit 79
full-body boost 140

G
generalised anxiety disorder 101
goal-setting 32, 34, 40, 41, 99, 100, 113
Goo goo pie 194
Granola 151, 157
gratitude 19, 28–9
Greek chicken with quinoa and salad 184
Greek spice mix 184
Green grainy slice 164
guilt 24, 34, 113
gym bonus set 116, 141
gym habits, unhelpful 117

H
Half Ironman 12
hamstring roll 133
happiness 25–6, 29, 98, 109, 111
health
  good 72, 74, 98, 107
  information 46, 61, 63
heart disease 81, 87
heartburn 82
Heavenly hummus 151, 175
heavy-weight exercise 52
high-intensity interval training (HIIT) 116
honey 81
hormonal changes 16, 28–9
hormones 15, 16, 19, 89
Hot cross bun jar 190
housework 32, 37
  see also chores
hunger 146, 152, 166
hydration 54, 93, 148
hyperflexion, of knees 56
hyperthyroidism 17
hypothyroidism 17

I
ice cream
  Dairy-free blueberry 201
  Dairy-free raspberry 202
Iced chocolate smoothie 170
independence 110–11
information, about health 46, 61, 63
ingredients, visualising 87–8
inner beauty 26, 95
Instagram 76
interval training 50
intuition 102–3
iron 80
irritable bowel syndrome 82
isolation 20–1, 25
ITB-band release 133, 142

J
jars
  Apple pie 190
  Blackberry, chocolate and cacao nib 191
  Hot cross bun 190
  Lemon meringue pie 191
jealousy 23, 103–4
journalling 19, 24, 41
judgement 95
juices 154
jump lunge 121
junk food 86–8, 91

K
knees 56

L
lactic acid 55, 61, 91, 93
leading lady role 113
leg muscles 52
leg-shaper 141
leggings 90
Lemon meringue pie jar 191
lethargy 82
  see also fatigue
life skills 32, 39
lists 43, 103
love 18, 25, 26, 28, 95, 111
lunches 149, 158–65
lunges 120–1
lying knee raise 131
lymph nodes 93
lymphatic drainage massage 55, 58–60
  Brazilian technique 58

M
macro goals 46
marriage 112
Mashed vegetables 151, 185
massage 55, 58–60, 93
meals
  frequency 82, 146, 148
  planning 148–51
meat 80
medication 74
meditation 64, 67
men's jobs 107
menstruation 14, 16
  training around 48
metabolism 11, 80, 82, 146, 152, 166
mind strengthening 70
mindfulness 29
  to manage fear 105
minerals 146
Miso soup 165
moisturiser 91
money 107
mood swings 82
morning routine 71
morning sickness 16
morning tea 148
motherhood 18, 26, 86, 100
  limitations 112
  self-sufficiency 21
  struggles 15, 16, 28–9
  and work 111
motivation 46–7, 50, 98, 99–100
movement 53, 64, 72, 74
muscles
  fatigue 52
  growth 51, 52, 56, 80
  leg muscles 52
  muscle tone 72
music, with a beat 47

N
Natvia 81
negativity 18–19, 29, 70, 89, 95, 106, 107, 110
'Nutella' layered sundae 202
nutrition 79, 83, 146

O
obesity 81
oestrogen 16
opportunities, for women 110, 111
optimism, strategies 106
overeating 82–3
ovulation 48

P
pain 14
peaceful spaces 66, 67
perfectionism 24
periods see menstruation
permission, seeking 111

personal chores 39
personal trainers 46, 52
Pesto pasta 185
physique 51
Picnic pie 151, 160
pigeon stretch 132
pilates 55, 61
placenta 16
plank tap 124
portion sizes 82, 147
positive reinforcement 39
positivity 26, 29, 70, 95, 106
post-natal depression 20–1, 28, 64
posture 56, 57, 89
praising others 95
pregnancy 14, 16, 18
premenstrual tension 16
priorities, setting 34, 40
produce, fresh 147
progesterone 16
protein 79, 80, 85
protein balls
   Apricot cashew 151, 169
   Chocolate 169
protein powder 80
protein shakes 93, 149
push-up climber 128
push-up deadlift press 129
push-up jump 128
push-ups 127–9

Q
quad roll 133
quick energy boost 140

R
Raw strawberry 'cheesecake' 196
red meat 80
reflux 21, 87
relaxation 64
reps per minute (RPM) 53
resistance training 51
respect 39
responsibilities, women's 23–4, 25
rewards 39
rice malt syrup 81
roughage 79
routine 71
running 15, 48

S
salads
   Clean green turkey 162
   Warm Italian 161
salmon fillets 147
scheduling 32, 33–5
science of the body 61, 63
seated groin and pigeon stretch 132
self-confidence 89, 103
self-doubt 102–3
self-talk, negative 18–19, 89, 107
selfishness 18
shoulder roll 133
side lunge 121
side-to-side squat jump 122
single motherhood 25, 110
skin 91
sleep 70, 71, 89
slices
   Energy slice 151, 156
   Envy slice 172
   Green grainy slice 164
smart phones 42
smoothies
   Caramel 170
   Fave smoothie 170
   Iced chocolate 170
   Spiced vanilla banana 157
snacks 166–75
   afternoon 149
snowball thinking 106
Snowsill-Froderio, Emma 13
social media 42, 76, 89
soft drinks 88
soup, Miso 165
speed ladder grit set 140
speed set 142
speed-weight circuits 52, 93
speed-weight exercise 116
spice mix, Greek 184
Spiced vanilla banana smoothie 157
spin 53
split squat 122
squat jump 123
squats 122–3
standing-press push up 127
Steady Fit program 116–17, 136–7
step-back lunge 120
step-ups 131
stevia 81
stimulants 64
stomach 82
stomach ache 87
strength training 51, 52
stress 33, 58, 63
   relieving 64, 66–7, 70, 74
stretches 55, 93, 118
stroke 81, 87
sugar 64, 76, 88, 92
   afternoon slump 80, 93, 149
   alternatives 81
   cravings 82, 186
   reducing intake 81
sumo squat 123
superman 130
superwomen 113
support network 20–1, 28
sweating 47, 90
Sweet crispy bread topped with yoghurt and fruit 168
Sweet potato pie 183
swimming 12, 64

T
T-stabilisation 129
taps/raises 124–5
taxation 107
technology 67
teenagers, chores 36
thyroxin 17
time management 42–3, 107
time-wasters 42
timers 43
tiredness *see* fatigue
toe-tap crunch 125
toe-tap leg raise 125
toxic food 86–7
toxic people 109–10
toxic waste 58, 61
toxins 55, 58, 61, 86–7, 91, 92, 93
training *see* fitness training
triathlons 12, 13, 14, 19

U
unwinding 67
upper body burner 141
upward-facing dog/energy stretch 132

V
V sit-up 129
values 40
Vegetable mash 151, 185
Vegie burgers 180
visualisation 41, 70
vitamin E 91
vitamins 146

W
walking 47, 64, 67
walking lunge 121
walkout 126
Warm Italian salad 161
warming up 118
water 54, 74, 85, 87, 92, 93, 148
water intoxication 54
weight control 50, 63, 75, 82
weight loss 53, 58, 80, 81, 116
weight loss promoters 85, 146
weight training 51
wellbeing 6, 16
wellness 55
whole-body function 58
whole body reshape 141
whole grains 79
Wholegrain bread 151, 174
wide-leg weight tap 124
work 66
work ethic 113
workouts
   core workout 140
   with friends 47
   tips 118
worry 101, 107
wrinkles 91

Y
yoga 55, 56, 61, 64, 93
youth 71

Z
Zucchini quiche 179

Index 207

Published in 2019 by Murdoch Books, an imprint of Allen & Unwin

Murdoch Books Australia
83 Alexander Street
Crows Nest NSW 2065
Phone: +61 (0)2 8425 0100
murdochbooks.com.au
info@murdochbooks.com.au

Murdoch Books UK
Ormond House
26–27 Boswell Street
London WC1N 3JZ
Phone: +44 (0) 20 8785 5995
murdochbooks.co.uk
info@murdochbooks.co.uk

For Corporate Orders & Custom Publishing, contact our Business Development Team at salesenquiries@murdochbooks.com.au.

Publisher: Kelly Doust
Editorial Manager: Julie Mazur Tribe
Design Manager and designer: Madeleine Kane
Editor: Andrea O'Connor
Production Director: Lou Playfair
Photography: Belinda Norton; except pages 153, 155, 159, 163, 167, 173, 177, 181, 187, 193, 197, 203 by Ainsley Johnstone; 27 by Samuel Scrimshaw; 65 by Ishan seefromthesky; 94 by Samsommer. Marble and speckled backgrounds used throughout by Rawpixel; white plaster background by Joanna Kosinska. Illustration on page 54 from iStock

Text © Belinda Norton 2019
The moral right of the author has been asserted.
Design © Murdoch Books 2019
Photography © Belinda Norton 2019, except pages 153, 155, 159, 163, 167, 173, 177, 181, 187, 193, 197, 203 © Ainsley Johnstone; and pages 27, 65, 94
Cover photography by Belinda Norton, except image on back cover (bottom left) by Ainsley Johnstone

All rights reserved. No part of this publication may be reproduced, stored in a retrieval system or transmitted in any form or by any means, electronic, mechanical, photocopying, recording or otherwise, without the prior written permission of the publisher.

A cataloguing-in-publication entry is available from the catalogue of the National Library of Australia at nla.gov.au.

ISBN 978 1 76052 408 1 Australia
ISBN 978 1 91163 203 0 UK

A catalogue record for this book is available from the British Library.

Colour reproduction by Splitting Image Colour Studio Pty Ltd, Clayton, Victoria
Printed by Hang Tai Printing Company Limited, China

The content presented in this book is meant for inspiration and informational purposes only. The purchaser of this book understands that the author is not a medical professional, and the information contained within this book is not intended to replace medical advice or meant to be relied upon to treat, cure, or prevent any disease, illness, or medical condition. It is understood that you will seek full medical clearance by a licensed physician before making any changes mentioned in this book. The author and publisher claim no responsibility to any person or entity for any liability, loss, or damage caused or alleged to be caused directly or indirectly as a result of the use, application, or interpretation of the material in this book.

MIX
Paper from responsible sources
FSC® C023121